VOLUME 90 • NUMBER 2 • SUMMER 2001

NATIONAL

CIVIC

REVIEW

MAKING CITIZEN DEMOCRACY WORK

IN THIS ISSUE

The State of Politics in America: Issues in Political Reform

T0358252

Christopher T. Gates
President, National Civic League

Robert Loper
Editor

A Publication of the National Civic League and Jossey-Bass

NATIONAL CIVIC REVIEW (ISSN 0027-9013) is published quarterly by Jossey-Bass, 350 Sansome Street, San Francisco, CA 94104-1342, and the National Civic League, 1445 Market Street, Suite 300, Denver, CO 80202-1717. NCL, founded in 1894 as the National Municipal League, advocates a new civic agenda to create communities that work for everyone. NCL is a 501(c)(3) nonprofit, nonpartisan educational association of individuals and organizations. NCL members have access to the information and services necessary to improve community life. For complete information, contact Derek Okubo, (303) 571-4343.

INDEXED in Public Affairs Information Service, ABC POL SCI, and Book Review Index.

SUBSCRIPTIONS are $50.00 per year for individuals and $83.00 per year for institutions. To order subscriptions, single issues, or reprints, please refer to the Ordering Information page at the back of this issue.

PERIODICALS postage paid at San Francisco, California, and at additional mailing offices. POSTMASTER: send address changes to National Civic Review, Jossey-Bass Inc., 350 Sansome Street, San Francisco, CA 94104-1342.

NCL MEMBERS send change of address to Debbie Gettings, National Civic League, 1445 Market Street, Suite 300, Denver, CO 80202-1717.

EDITORIAL CORRESPONDENCE should be sent to Robert Loper, National Civic League, 1319 F Street NW, Suite 204, Washington, DC, 20004.

www.josseybass.com

LETTERS TO THE EDITOR. *National Civic Review* welcomes letters to the editor. Write to *National Civic Review,* 1319 F Street, Suite 204, Washington, DC, 20004, or send e-mail to robert@ncldc.org. Please include your name, address, and telephone number.

CONTENTS

NOTE FROM THE PRESIDENT

Election 2000 put voting reform on the national agenda. The inability to ensure that all duly registered voters could vote and that all votes could be counted was unsettling to everyone. Such problems have direct implications for the legitimacy of our political system.

A flurry of activity followed the fiasco in Florida. Numerous studies were launched and commissions were formed; lawsuits were filed in a number of jurisdictions. Election reform measures have been introduced in legislatures across the country, most notably in Florida itself where legislators agreed to ban punch card machines, provide money for new voting machines, and establish uniform standards for vote recounts.

While it is too early to discern the ultimate impact of these and other reforms, it is easy enough to identify the fault lines separating different points of view. State officials, protective of their prerogative in electoral matters, desire federal financing with minimal federal oversight. While stopping short of imposing uniform standards, Congress will nonetheless be reluctant to appropriate funds without attaching some strings. On the partisan front, Democrats focus more on identifying and removing barriers to voting while Republicans raise concerns over voter fraud. These crosscutting currents have already prompted predictions that Election 2002 will be more like its predecessor than was originally hoped.

Years ago, Leslie Gelb wrote an article (and later co-authored a book) on the Vietnam War in which he argued that our involvement was not the result of a foreign policy breakdown but rather was a product of how the system worked. It is useful to think of Florida and Election 2000 in the same way. Election officials have long known about the kinds of problems that surfaced last year. The not-so-secret little fact about the way we conduct elections in this country is that we do not devote sufficient resources to the process to avoid the results that we saw recently. There are a host of reasons for this, some of which are related to the allocation of authority in our system of government and some of which bear the marks of partisan maneuvering for electoral advantage. In other words, the outcome of last year's election should be seen not as an aberration but as an expression of how our political system currently works. And that means that voting reform is only one topic in a wider debate that we should be having about political reform in general. There are discrete problems in our voting systems, such as antiquated and error-prone voting machinery, which can be remedied by improvements in the mechanics of how votes are cast and counted. But just as new technology is not the only change needed to improve how we vote, a conversation that just focuses on reforming our electoral system will not address all the areas in which reforms are needed.

This issue of the *National Civic Review* contributes to that wider discussion. Before the problems in Florida drew attention to the need for electoral reform, the campaign finance system was the principal focus of reform measures. A number of articles in this issue of the *Review* address the topic of campaign finance reform. Senate passage of the McCain-Feingold bill presages what would be the most significant advance on the federal level since the creation of the modern campaign finance system after Watergate in the mid-1970s. But there have been a number of developments at the state and local levels, ranging from Clean Money/Clean Election agreements to partial public financing systems, that go even further in restraining the potentially corrupting effects of campaign finance. This disparity between what has been accomplished to date at the federal versus the state and local levels supports an observation about contemporary politics and the prospects for political change. Reform efforts at the local level are needed to build momentum for political change at the national level.

The National Civic League is committed to this proposition and works in communities across the country to promote innovative political reform. Partisan conflict and stalemate at the federal level make reform efforts at the state and local levels all the more important. In various communities there is already a movement toward multisectoral, collaborative decision making in which all parties—the private sector, the public sector, nonprofit organizations, and citizen groups—come together to the table to solve problems. This emerging model of governance holds great promise for communities in tackling issues of local concern. But it is incumbent upon us all to find ways of connecting the energy we see at the local level to the national debate over priorities and policies.

We need to identify and ameliorate barriers to political participation at the same time that we develop new means for encouraging civic engagement at all levels. With generous assistance from the Ford Foundation, the Open Society Institute, and the Carnegie Corporation, the NCL's New Politics Program works to accomplish these goals. The reform proposals advanced here address a number of these important issues, and it is hoped that this issue of the *Review* will stimulate further discussion and activity. Electoral and political reform issues have attained a new salience following last year's election. This opportunity to make progress should not go unrealized.

CHRISTOPHER T. GATES
PRESIDENT, NATIONAL CIVIC LEAGUE

Citizen Democracy

Dorothy Ridings

As this article was being written, electoral reform proposals were in early flower in Washington. Senate passage of the McCain-Feingold bill presaged new possibilities for reforming our political system. No less than those of baseball fans, the hopes of political reformers spring eternal. Yet whatever the effects of any legislation from this round of reform, we will still have cause to be concerned about the state of democracy in America. This is said not to disparage the current reforms but rather as an invitation to consider what we want reform to accomplish.

The most widespread sentiment about politics in our country is perhaps general dissatisfaction. A low regard for the political arts is not new, but events during the most recent election cycle do not seem to have redounded to anyone's credit. Whatever else may be said of it, the Florida debacle made the need for reform clear to all.

This issue of the *National Civic Review* contains a number of essays calling for structural reforms to our political system. These include proposals to do away with the electoral college, make free airtime available to qualified candidates, eliminate barriers to ballot access for third parties, and expand the use of alternate voting systems such as instant runoff voting or proportional representation. Campaign finance reform is a fundamental issue in its own right, and the recent history of reform efforts at the local, state, and federal levels is recounted in this issue as well. These and other proposals should receive serious attention and debate.

Given the well-publicized problems with ballot design and voting machines, it is likely that changes will be made in these areas as well. Among the most promising improvements already garnering widespread attention are voting machines that give voters an opportunity to correct their ballots before they turn them in. A number of jurisdictions already use some form of this technology and others are sure to adopt it, as the financing becomes available.

But in the midst of this debate and activity there is another level of concern that must not go unattended. We have become largely inured to a rate of voter turnout that does us no credit as a democratic republic. Here too we do not lack for proposals about how to boost a turnout rate that hovers near 50 percent for a presidential election and slumps to slightly over one-third of the eligible voters during a midterm election. Suggested reforms range from various measures for making registration less cumbersome to making Election Day a national holiday, holding elections on the weekend, or instituting uniform poll closings. These ideas propose reasonable remedies, and practical trials are already under way in a number of states and localities. But as for efforts to control the role of money or make ballot access more equitable, there is a sense in which these reform proposals address the symptoms rather than the causes of problems afflicting our democracy.

Over the last quarter century, certain political trends at the federal level have converged, giving rise to a structure of self-reinforcing elements. The process described by Joe McGinniss in *The Selling of the President 1968* has metastasized into a system in which individual candidates no longer merely contend with their political rivals but find themselves in competition with all other advertised products, each clamoring for a dwindling share of the citizen consumer's attention. The features of this system can be quickly stylized, and without caricature. A political campaign is a highly professional operation, relying on sophisticated polling, focus group testing, and targeted marketing, orchestrated by independent political consultants for hire. The escalating importance of political advertising necessitates an unrelenting focus on raising the vast sums required. The clangor of negative advertising produces an effect, like Gresham's law, on political discourse whereby the bad drowns out the good. The media have moved from being profilers of the action to becoming participants within it.

The cumulative impact of these developments has reduced the cohesion and importance of political parties, elevated the role of money and the special interests that provide it, and left much of the eligible voting population feeling ignored and overlooked. Tune in, turn off, and drop out has become the new mantra.

This is, in some sense at least, how the situation appears at the federal level. The reforms advocated by the contributors to this issue of *NCR* would, if enacted, have a significant positive impact on many of these problems. Reducing barriers to political participation and constraining the role of special-interest campaign contributions can create a more level playing field. But the most important potential effects of these reforms are likely to go unrealized if, after the gates have been opened, people don't even bother to enter the arena.

A familiar strain of criticism reproves citizens for not voting and decries the level of apparent political apathy across the country. However, as the response to offensive speech is said to be more speech rather than restrictions on free speech, the remedy for what ails our democracy could be more democracy rather than admonitions about citizen responsibility, no matter how well intentioned. In fact, contrary to the view that sees politics as beset by widespread citizen apathy, there is evidence that a new model of politics is finding favor among citizens at the local level. This model represents a new flowering of citizen democracy, or participatory democracy as it has also been called.

At the heart of the new model of politics described by the term *citizen democracy* is a shift in concern from government (what public officials do) to governance (the collective ways in which private citizens, the public sector, the private sector, and nonprofit groups work together to solve problems). Because much of the citizen involvement with issues of governance occurs at the community level and is manifested in ways that are not overtly political in a traditional sense, it is perhaps easy to consider this activity as being secondary to national political concerns. But to overlook what is happening at this level risks misunderstanding the changing nature of contemporary political activity and its significance for political reform measures.

The incipient rise of citizen democracy at the local level is the result of numerous factors, which I cannot hope to detail here. Among the most significant, however, are the shift in locus of government action from the federal to the state and local levels, the relative insufficiency of government capacity and resources to solve a number of social problems, and the increasing disaffection of citizens with what they see as a broken political system. Both major political parties have proclaimed the end of the era of big government. The devolution of authority to state governments has been driven in part by recognition of policy innovations at the state level. But there has also been a measure of stalemate at the federal level that has resulted in state and local governments assuming de facto responsibility that in many cases may be incommensurate with available resources. However, the factor behind the movement toward a "small-p politics" of local volunteerism and community involvement that I stress here is the response by citizens to a political system that they view with diminished trust and confidence.

Seen from the perspective of traditional politics—the "capital-P politics" of campaigns and elections—this response looks very much like a decision to opt out. Surveys document that voters are not well informed about many issues, and the percentage of citizens engaged in such traditional political activities as writing letters, working on a political campaign, making a campaign donation, or even voting is not encouraging. There is a conventional difference of opinion on this state of affairs that shares the common premise that voters are shirking their civic responsibility. One side holds that citizens are apathetic and their behavior is therefore deplorable. The other prefers to see citizens as complacent; though withholding rebuke, it agrees that their behavior is not admirable. But for some segment of the population, it is possible to argue that the motivating impulses for their disengagement are anger and frustration and that their response, if seen clearly, is in some measure perfectly rational.

This segment comprises individuals who, though having turned away from traditional politics, have nevertheless not turned entirely away from civic engagement. Where once party identification might have led them into traditional political activity, their desire to make a difference leads them into activism of another sort. Think of these individuals as the political cousins of the rational agents so beloved by economic theorists. Frustrated by a political system that they regard as being more responsive to other interests, if not altogether dysfunctional, they see a high degree of involvement with this system as an irrational expenditure of their time and money. Instead, they focus their energy on issues where they believe their involvement can have an impact.

This attitudinal shift and redirection of attention has found fertile opportunity for engagement at the community level. Many local governments lack sufficient resources to solely address the range of needs that exist within their communities. When this occurs, others step up. Whether creating and staffing a volunteer after-school program to offer supplemental teaching to students, initiating a crime prevention program in the neighborhood, or participating in developing a land-use policy, individuals across the country have formed local organizations to provide important services in concert with government programs.

It is fair to ask how significant this type of activity is; the best answer we have at present is that we are not sure. It is, however, important to keep in mind that the forms of political activity are historical and evolve over time under the impress of changing conditions and opportunities. At least at the local level, if not at the state level as well, there is evidence that a new model of multisectoral decision making is emerging wherein multiple stakeholders are coming to the table. For many issues, authority and responsibility are more diffuse than before, and decisions on them now require a greater degree of consensus among a wider group of people and interests for effective implementation. Changing citizen attitudes and the inability of local governments to unilaterally resolve complex issues have redefined the contours of the political commons, that is, the social landscape in which individuals and volunteer associations play a public role.

Invigoration of citizen democracy at the local level presents both a challenge and an opportunity for politics as usual. The politics of federal campaigns and elections will always be significant, and in truth disengagement is not a viable option in the long run. But as the political system at the federal level comes to seem more and more like a rigged game among ever-fewer players, there is an increasing cost measured in needs unrecognized and goals unrealized. Citizen concern with issues that directly affect daily life in their communities is a laudatory activity that no one would want to discourage. But engagement at this level alone is not likely to be sufficient even for many of the issues that attract citizen involvement. We need to develop ways to connect the two worlds of politics, drawing citizens back into a reconstructed political system in which they have trust and confidence because they are actively engaged in affecting outcomes.

If, as I suggest, part of what animates citizen democracy at the local level is the combination of frustration with traditional politics and desire to improve community conditions, then we may have reason to be optimistic about building the necessary bridges between small-p and capital-P politics. The key is to change the incentives facing individuals as they decide whether and how to commit their time and energy on issues of public importance. It is reasonable to expect that community activists will experience a mixture of success and frustration at the local level. Some issues are more recalcitrant to community-based solution than others. Some groups in some areas, as is already happening, will broaden the scope of their efforts, connecting with other organizations working on the same or allied issues.

As this process develops, it is imperative that we reform governmental structures across all levels, implementing many of the measures suggested elsewhere in this journal. When citizens who are engaged in their local communities, building citizen democracy issue-by-issue and project-by-project, recognize that the larger political system has become more fair and responsive, we will not need to worry about their entering the arena. We will find them already on the field.

Dorothy Ridings is the chair of the National Civic League and the president and chief executive officer of the Council on Foundations.

Federal Campaign Finance Reform: The Long and Winding Road

Scott Harshbarger, Edwin Davis

On February 26, 2001, Senator John McCain (R-Ariz.) spoke at the University of Oklahoma to an enthusiastic crowd of fifteen hundred people from the university and surrounding communities. Oklahoma was one stop in a series of events throughout the country that the senator and his reform ally, Senator Russell Feingold (D-Wis.), were conducting to put pressure on their fellow senators to vote for campaign finance reform legislation. Given the current prospects for such legislation, McCain's stop in Oklahoma was perhaps a symbolic linkage between the beginning and the completion of a reform effort that began in the mid-1980s. He was invited to Oklahoma by the president of the university, David Boren. A former Democratic U.S. senator from Oklahoma, Boren was a key figure in starting the recent reform process.

This article traces the series of reform fights in Congress over the past fifteen years, as the problems in the campaign finance system altered and as a changing cast of members of Congress took up the torch of reform with proposals responding to the different problems. The article is intended to offer some perspective for those who first began paying attention to campaign finance reform during the 2000 presidential campaign, when McCain brought the issue to the nation's attention and made it a priority in the crowded agenda of the nation's capital.

Overview: Watergate and Beyond

In 1974, in the wake of the Watergate scandal, the landmark Federal Election Campaign Amendments (FECA) were enacted, setting contribution limits for all federal campaigns and establishing a system of public financing and spending limits for presidential campaigns. In 1976, Congress passed legislation making changes to the 1974 act in response to the Supreme Court's *Buckley* v. *Valeo* decision, which upheld FECA but struck down some of its provisions. In the late 1970s, efforts to pass public financing for congressional campaigns were turned back, and in 1979 Congress enacted some minor changes to

FECA. It was not until 1985 that Common Cause and its reform allies in Congress were able to get Congress to vote on significant reform legislation.

From 1979 until 1985, there were no significant reform votes. This break was in some sense artificial; reformers did not totally retreat from their efforts. Rather, the early years of Ronald Reagan's presidency (he was elected in 1980) were not conducive to reform, and some of the groups pushing reform became engaged in other issues.

Changing Problems: PACs and Soft Money

During the period from the mid-1980s to the turn of the new century, the landscape of the nation's campaign finance system changed profoundly. These changes determined which reform proposals were brought before Congress. In general, reform advocates attempted to focus on the worst problems in the system at the time, but they were also influenced by their view of what could be passed in the Senate or House.

In the mid-1980s, the problem at the top of the agenda was the influence of political action committee (PAC) contributions, particularly their role in protecting incumbents in the House of Representatives. Under FECA, PACs may contribute up to $5,000 to a candidate in each election. Although a corporation, union, or other organization may establish a PAC and pay for its administrative expenses, all contributions made by the PAC must come from funds that are voluntarily contributed by employees of the corporation or members of the union.

The recent reform effort started during Reagan's presidency with a proposal of a fairly simple limit on the amount of PAC contributions that candidates could accept. Over the period from 1988 to 1994, when Democrats were in control of both houses of Congress, public financing measures were a key part of the reform agenda in Congress. Common Cause and other reform groups championed various forms of public financing: matching grants, communications vouchers, and free or reduced-cost TV time. The Republican takeover of Congress in 1994 effectively marginalized public financing as a near-term reform goal. It remains a key reform in many states and a long-term goal at the federal level.

More recently, since 1995, McCain and Feingold in the Senate and Representatives Christopher Shays (R-Conn.) and Martin Meehan (D-Mass.) in the House have focused their efforts on the most egregious problem in the campaign finance system today: soft money. The term refers to unlimited donations from corporations, labor unions, and wealthy individuals to the political parties, which in turn funnel the money into federal campaigns. Much of this money would be illegal if given to candidates directly, such as money from corporations and labor unions. Although a corporation or union may establish a PAC, it is prohibited from making donations directly from its treasury to a party's federal account and to a candidate.

The soft-money system had its origins in a 1978 Federal Election Commission ruling, but it was not until the 1988 campaign that soft money became a major factor in elections. Soft-money contributions went from an estimated $19 million in the 1980 election to $45 million in 1988 but then soared to $463 million in the 2000 election. Soft money so dominates the campaign finance system that without eliminating it, there is little hope that other reforms will be at all effective. As E. J. Dionne, political columnist for the *Washington Post,* writes, "McCain and Feingold are . . . proposing a first step that doesn't go far enough, but is absolutely necessary if other steps are to be taken."[1] Indeed, the wave of soft money has effectively obliterated virtually every campaign finance reform of the past century: the 1907 ban on corporate contributions to candidates, the 1947 ban on labor treasury contributions to candidates, the 1974 contribution limits, and the 1974 spending and public financing system for presidential campaigns.

2001

As this article was being written, the Senate was considering the McCain-Feingold bill. S. 27, the Bipartisan Campaign Finance Reform Act of 2001, bans soft money and restricts "phony" issue ads run by corporations and unions. Reformers have several reasons to be optimistic that the legislation will be enacted. McCain made the issue of campaign finance reform salient in the campaign this past fall, and five opponents of reform were replaced with new senators who are likely to support it. Because of the new senators, reformers now have the support of sixty senators, enough to overcome a filibuster, a key procedural obstacle during this cycle of reform.[2]

Although the Senate elections brought new support in Congress for reform, the results of the presidential election may have placed a major obstacle in its path. Al Gore pledged to make campaign finance reform his first priority. Although President George W. Bush has not indicated what action he will ultimately take, he has not expressed support for the McCain-Feingold bill. If Bush reprises his father's 1992 veto of reform legislation, sixty-seven votes in the Senate would be needed to pass McCain-Feingold into law.

Finally, the real possibility that the McCain-Feingold bill might pass this time around has attracted new opposition. Many Democrats are worried that the end of soft money and an increase in the limits on hard money would favor the Republicans. The Republican national party raises far more hard money than the Democratic party: $345 million to $207 million in the 1999–2000 election cycle. Additionally, organizations ideologically compatible with the Republican party pour far more money into independent spending. Therefore, according to this view, without the outlet of soft money, big money in politics would go disproportionately to independent groups to buy so-called sham issue ads, campaign ads masquerading as issue discussion. Labor unions, which were quiet during reform fights in recent years, have stepped in this time, expressing serious opposition to elements of the McCain-Feingold bill.

Federal Campaign Finance Reform:
An In-Depth Retrospective

Reform of the federal campaign finance system has proven to be difficult for a number of reasons. Although perceptions of relative advantage color each major party's view of reform, incumbents in both parties are often reluctant to alter a system that they have benefited from. Reform proponents have also had to adapt their proposals to changing political conditions, not the least of which has been the change in party control of the White House and Congress over the course of the contemporary reform cycle. This section details the legislative struggles over campaign finance reform since 1985.

Boren-Goldwater: Ninety-Ninth Congress, 1985–86. During his time in the Senate, David Boren, a moderately conservative Democrat, developed great respect for the icon of conservative Republicans, Barry Goldwater of Arizona. In 1985, Boren asked Goldwater to team up with him on a reform bill he was planning to introduce. For Goldwater, allying himself with a moderate Democrat in a fight against special interests was a break with the leadership of the Republican party but was in keeping with his view that limited government should serve the people.

Boren and Goldwater, joined by a bipartisan group of Senators, took their proposal to the Senate floor in December 1985.[3] The focus of the bill, S. 1806, the Campaign Finance Reform Act Boren-Goldwater, was an aggregate limit on PAC contributions, that is, an overall limit on the dollar amount that each candidate could accept in PAC contributions (the amount of the limit for senators was set by a formula based on voting-age population, while House candidates would be limited to $100,000). On December 3, by a vote of 7–84, the Senate rejected a motion to table the Boren-Goldwater bill. The bill had been offered as an amendment to S. 655, the Low-Level Radioactive Waste Compact; that bill was pulled from consideration after the vote because the leadership feared Boren-Goldwater would pass as an amendment to the otherwise noncontroversial measure. Several months later, the pair from Oklahoma and Arizona brought the bill to a vote again, this time winning passage by a vote of 69–30 on August 12, 1986.

But the Boren-Goldwater bill, passed late in the Ninety-ninth Congress, did not go any further—a harbinger of the next fourteen years of reform efforts. The House did not act on similar legislation, and the Boren-Goldwater bill died.

Eight Cloture Votes: One-Hundredth Congress, 1987–88. After the Ninety-ninth Congress, Goldwater retired from the Senate, ending his thirty-year career there. But Boren had a new partner as he faced the next round of reform in the Senate. The majority leader, Robert Byrd (D-W. Va.), teamed up with Boren and became one of the leaders of the effort. Byrd, who at that time had been in the Senate for nearly thirty years, was the grandmaster of Senate rules and procedures; his willingness to lead the fight was a major boost for reform. Byrd and Boren sponsored S. 2, the Senatorial Election Campaign Act, a bill that included spending limits, reduced-cost broadcasting and mail rates, soft-money restrictions, and an aggregate PAC limit.

The proposed aggregate limit on PAC contributions that candidates could accept was based on a percentage of the spending limit (which was itself based on the voting-age population for each state). In S. 2, the limit on PAC contributions was 30 percent of the spending limit, up to $825,000. In the reform fights over PAC limits, reformers supported PAC limits in the range of 20 percent of the spending limit, while PAC supporters tried to eliminate the limit or negotiate a figure up to 50 percent of the spending limit.

In one of the most extraordinary exhibitions of perseverance on the Senate floor, from June 1987 to February 1988 Byrd led the Senate through eight unsuccessful cloture votes to end a filibuster.[4] Byrd was able to muster fifty-three votes for cloture in the eighth and final attempt. But even his prodigious political power and parliamentary skill could not overcome the stubborn opposition of reform opponents (among them Minority Leader Robert Dole, R-Kans.).

Just before the final cloture vote, Byrd, averting an attempt to adjourn the Senate for lack of a quorum raised, used an arcane rule to ask that the Senate sergeant at arms be instructed to arrest the absent senators and bring them into the chamber. Senator Robert Packwood (R-Oreg.) was carried, peacefully but forcefully, onto the Senate floor.

The multiple cloture vote strategy failed, but Byrd and others believed the prolonged fight focused media attention on campaign finance reform and put the issue firmly on the national agenda.

In the House, the long dry spell for reformers continued. Representatives David Obey (D-Wis.), James Leach (R-Iowa), and Mike Synar (D-Okla.) introduced H.R. 2717, the Federal Election Campaign Act, which included spending limits, public matching funds, and an aggregate PAC limit. The House did not act on it.

The Big Stall: 101st Congress, 1989–90. The 101st Congress was a frustrating time for reform advocates. For the first time since 1974, both the House and Senate passed comprehensive reform bills, but passage was delayed until late in the session, leaving only a few weeks for a conference committee to meet and resolve differences between the two bills. Opponents were able to block any effort to convene a conference, and once again reform foundered on the shoals of delay.

The Senate passed S. 137, Senatorial Campaign Amendments, by a vote of 59–40 on August 1, 1990. Majority Leader George Mitchell (D-Maine), along with Boren, Byrd, and others, sponsored the bill. S. 137 included spending limits; TV vouchers; reduced-cost TV, radio, and mail; a ban on PAC contributions (with a backup provision setting an aggregate limit should the ban be ruled unconstitutional); and soft-money restrictions. Common Cause strongly supported the legislation.

As the Senate was once again moving ahead to pass reform legislation, the Democrat-controlled House was struggling. Reluctant Democrats patched together a reform measure with virtually no Republican input or support. The bill, H.R. 5400, Campaign Cost Reduction and Election Reform Act, passed by a vote of 255–155 on August 3, 1990. H.R. 5400 included spending limits; reduced-cost TV, radio, and mail; tax credits for in-state contributions; a 50 percent aggregate PAC "limit"; and soft-money restrictions. The votes on this bill were the first in the House on campaign finance since 1979. Common Cause offered lukewarm support for the final measure, hoping that a conference with the Senate would result in stronger legislation.

During House consideration of the bill, Common Cause supported an amendment offered by Synar and Obey, which included a 40 percent PAC limit, spending limits, public matching funds, and lower individual contribution limits. The amendment was defeated on August 3, 1990, by a vote of 122–128, as Republicans, in a parliamentary maneuver intended to kill the overall bill, voted "present."

Bush Veto: 102nd Congress, 1991–92. In the 102nd Congress, reformers suffered yet another twist of the knife. This time, a bill was sent to the president's desk for signature, but it was all a thinly veiled ruse. Many members of Congress who voted for the measure did so knowing that the president would veto the bill and that there were not enough votes to override the veto.

At the outset of this Congress, Boren teamed up with a formidable set of Democratic senators: Majority Leader Mitchell; Wendell Ford (Ky.), chair of the Rules Committee; Robert Byrd, now chair of the powerful Appropriations Committee; and Carl Levin (Mich.), a key strategic leader for reform. This group and others sponsored S. 3, the Senate Election Ethics Act, which included spending limits, public financing, aggregate PAC limits, and soft-money restrictions. The public financing provisions included communications vouchers, low-cost mailing, and discounted TV rates. S. 3 passed the Senate by a vote of 56–42 on May 23, 1991.

The House Democratic leadership developed legislation similar to S.3. This bill, H.R. 3750, the House of Representatives Spending Limit and Election Reform Act, included spending limits and an aggregate PAC limit (public financing provisions were struck from the bill before it reached the House floor). The bill passed the House by a vote of 273–156 on November 25, 1991. Yet the strong support of Democrats was misleading; they knew that Bush intended to veto campaign finance reform legislation passed by a Democratic Congress. For those Democrats who secretly opposed reform, this vote was an easy way out: a way to be for reform publicly, all the while knowing no reform would be signed into law, and they could later campaign against Bush as the antireform candidate.

The House adopted the S. 3 conference report by a vote of 259–165 on April 9, 1992. The Senate passed the S. 3 conference report by a vote of 56–42 on April 30, 1992. On May 9, 1992 Bush vetoed the bill, saying, "We do not need . . . a taxpayer-financed incumbent protection plan."[5] Four days later, in a predictable and anticlimactic vote, the Senate failed to override the veto by a vote of 57–42 (nine votes short of the required two-thirds majority). Common Cause supported the legislation but did so with a sense of resignation over the foreseeable outcome.

Clinton, Foley, and McConnell: 103rd Congress, 1993–94. On Inauguration Day, January 20, 1993, President Bill Clinton told the nation in his inaugural speech: "This beautiful Capital, like every capital since the dawn of civilization, is often a place of intrigue and calculation. . . . And so I say to all of you here: let us resolve to reform our politics so that power and privilege no longer shout down the voice of the people. . . . Let us give this Capital back to the people to whom it belongs."[6] But the reform sentiment reflected in the speech proved to be short-lived and insincere. Within weeks, in meetings with the Democratic leadership in Congress, Clinton readily acceded to their view that campaign finance reform would hurt Democrats' ability to hold onto their majorities in Congress. Over the next eight years, Clinton occasionally included support of reform in his speeches but never made any significant effort to push for campaign finance reform legislation in Congress.

This failure to support reform was never more critical than in the 103rd Congress, when both the Senate and House passed sweeping reform legislation, including spending limits, public resources in the form of low-cost TV and other communications resources, soft-money restrictions, and PAC limits.

The Senate passed S. 3, the Congressional Spending Limit and Election Reform Act, by a vote of 60–38 on June 17, 1993. The bill's principal sponsors were Boren and Mitchell. S. 3 included spending limits, low-cost TV time and mail rates, a PAC ban, and a soft-money ban. Common Cause supported the legislation.

The House again passed a broad but weaker version of the Senate bill. H.R. 3, the Campaign Spending Limit and Election Reform Act, passed by a vote of 255–175 on November 22, 1993. H.R. 3 included spending limits, an aggregate PAC limit, communications vouchers (without a funding mechanism), and soft-money restrictions. Representative Sam Gejdenson (D-Conn.) and the Democratic leadership sponsored the bill.

The House bill was less attractive to reformers, but there was a realistic possibility that a House-Senate conference committee would produce a strong reform package. Unfortunately, over the year remaining in the 103rd Congress after the House passed its bill in November 1993, the Democrats (who controlled Congress and the White House) stalled and refused to push hard for a conference. Both reform bills died.

The Democrats were not the only reason reform died in the 103rd Congress. Another key figure in this protracted stall was a long-time opponent of reform who was emerging as the Darth Vader of Congressional reform battles. Republican Senator Mitch McConnell of Kentucky used the Senate's sixty-vote filibuster weapon to block any efforts to move the Senate legislation to conference.

The opposition to reform by a range of Democrats and Republicans in Congress—as well as White House passivity—showed how thin and brittle majority votes for reform are. There are many members of Congress who publicly support reform and vote for good legislation but then stand by and allow opponents to defeat any reform effort.

Republicans Take Over: 104th Congress, 1995–96. When the Republicans took over the House in 1995 after forty years of Democratic control, the leadership of the reform effort shifted to bipartisan groups that formed in both the House and Senate. In the House, moderate Republican Shays had already developed ties with liberal Democrat Meehan and other Democrats on a number of issues and began working with this bipartisan group on a gift ban, lobby disclosure rules, and campaign finance reform legislation. This coalition was critical to passage of gift limits and lobby disclosure rules in 1995 and continued to push its reform agenda, developing legislation and expanding the bipartisan coalition. The efforts of Republicans in this reform coalition were met with hostility from the newly empowered Republican House leadership.

In June 1995, campaign finance reform seemed to get a boost at an unusual joint public appearance by House Speaker Newt Gingrich (R-Ga.) and President Clinton in New Hampshire. When the speaker was asked a question about reform, he responded by proposing a commission. Clinton and Gingrich reached toward each other and shook hands, agreeing to establish a campaign finance reform commission. The proposal later died, but the photo of the handshake continued to appear in the media as reform measures floundered in the 104th Congress.

The House coalition's first test on campaign finance reform was playing defense to defeat a Republican-leadership-backed campaign finance bill. The bill, H.R. 3820, was designed to take the reform issue from the Democrats. Introduced by Rep. Bill Thomas (R-Calif.) and later revised when it met with widespread opposition (from Common Cause among others), the bill featured a mish-mash of proposals including a paycheck protection provision[7] that guaranteed Democratic opposition. The bill was defeated by a vote of 162–259 on July 25, 1996.

The Republican leadership was responding to the successful effort by Shays and Meehan to forge a bipartisan coalition behind real reform. H.R. 2566, the Bipartisan Clean Congress Act (supported by Common Cause), was sponsored by Shays, Meehan, conservative Linda Smith (R-Wash.), and Benjamin Cardin (D-Md.). The legislation included spending limits, a PAC ban (with an aggregate PAC limit as a backup), and a ban on soft money. The House did not consider the bill, but its introduction forced the leadership to consider an issue it had no interest in addressing.

Meanwhile, in the Senate, another cloture vote failed, but a new bipartisan coalition was forming. S. 1219, the Senate Campaign Finance Reform Act, was stopped on the Senate floor by a vote of 54–46 on June 25, 1996—six votes short of the sixty needed to end the filibuster. The bill was supported by Common Cause and sponsored by McCain, Feingold, and Fred Thompson (R-Tenn.).

The bill included spending limits, free and reduced-cost TV time, a PAC ban (with an aggregate PAC limit as a backup), and a ban on soft money.

As in the House, this new bipartisan set of Senate sponsors came together working on a successful effort to pass a gift ban rule. McCain, Feingold, and a few other Senators took on an issue close to the hearts and pocketbooks of members of Congress: gifts, meals, and travel paid for by lobbyists. Feingold, who had served in a legislature operating under one of the toughest gift bans in any state, was ready to bring this key reform to Congress. McCain, a politician with a reputation for honesty and forthrightness, had a brush with scandal when he became embroiled in the savings and loan debacle known as the Keating Five affair. Although in the end the Senate did not reprimand McCain, the matter did leave a stain on his career and, in the view of some observers, heightened his interest in reform.

Summer of '98: 105th Congress, 1997–98. During and after the 1996 election, there were numerous stories in the media—and investigations begun in the Justice Department—regarding violations of campaign finance laws, many of them involving soft-money contributions. In late 1996, Common Cause called on the Justice Department to investigate soft-money abuses by the Democratic and Republican parties. In a letter to the Attorney General, Common Cause said that the violations of campaign finance law that occurred during the 1996 presidential election were the most massive since the Watergate scandal.

After more than a decade of the Senate taking the lead, in 1998 the leading edge of reform efforts shifted to the House. In a legislative battle playing out over several weeks in the summer of 1998, reformers skillfully negotiated an obstacle course set up by the House leadership to thwart reform and passed the Shays-Meehan soft-money ban, a bill that also included restrictions on phony issue ads.

Washington insiders all have stories to tell of titanic legislative fights over issues broad (for example, Social Security, defense spending) and narrow (such as ethanol tax incentives) that brought out the best in legislators and serve as case studies of how (or how not) to move legislation through Congress. This was one of those moments.

On April 4, 1998, the authoritative journal on Congress, *Congressional Quarterly,* declared the "year's last gasp for comprehensive campaign finance legislation"[8] was the defeat of a sham reform bill brought to the floor by the Republican leadership. The leadership had hoped to head off consideration of the Shays-Meehan legislation by offering a package with elements that would both appeal to and repel both sides on the issue. Their strategy failed, and the bill was defeated by an overwhelming vote of 74 to 337 on March 30, with every Democrat voting against the bill.

Shays, Meehan, and their allies were not ready to give up and continued an effort to bypass normal House procedures for considering legislation. Under a process called a discharge petition, reformers gathered more than 200 signatures of members who supported bringing the reform legislation to the House floor without approval of the leadership or the powerful Rules Committee. As reformers were about to gather the required 218 signatures (a majority of the 435 members of the body), Speaker Gingrich, an adamant foe of reform, headed off the process and agreed to allow the House to consider reform legislation.

But the leadership had not totally thrown in the towel. They devised a procedure that would delay passage of a bill in the House until late in the summer, leaving little time for the Senate to take up the bill. The leadership set a rule—the procedure under which legislation is considered—that allowed opportunities for nearly every possible opposing or undermining measure to be voted on by the House.

Over the course of the summer, from June 13 until August 6, the House considered a series of amendments and substitute bills for Shays-Meehan. Reformers beat back every "killer" and "poison pill" amendment, including measures designed to make the bill likely to be thrown out by the courts, a proposal to substitute a commission study for the bill, a paycheck protection amendment opposed by labor unions and designed to undermine Democratic support for the bill, and measures to repeal campaign finance laws in favor of a disclosure-only system.

Shays, Meehan, and their small bipartisan group of allies were faced with a House leadership totally opposed to reform and determined to place every possible obstacle in their path. Day by day, night by night, Shays and Meehan fought back competing amendments and bills with skillful, knowledgeable debate and legislative acumen. They were able to rally their troops at each crucial vote and defeat amendments that would have undermined critical provisions of their bill or would have splintered the bipartisan coalition they had painstakingly put together.

In the end, after substitute bills were defeated or withdrawn by their sponsors, the Shays-Meehan measure was passed by a vote of 237 to 186. The vote made the Shays-Meehan bill the last bill standing after the long fight; subsequently the House passed H.R. 2183 (now wholly amended by the Shays-Meehan bill) by a vote of 252 to 179 on August 6, 1998.

The Shays-Meehan triumph in the House was a victory for the future—one that put a majority of the House on record and ensured passage of similar legislation in the next Congress. But the victory celebration was muted by the reality that reformers could not reach the sixty votes needed to break a filibuster in the Senate.

The Senate followed a path similar to those of previous Congresses with a series of cloture votes. The latest version of McCain-Feingold was S. 25, the Bipartisan Campaign Finance Reform Act, which included a soft-money ban and restrictions on phony issue ads. With the leadership of Minority Leader Tom Daschle (D-S. Dak.), McCain and Feingold forced cloture votes on the measure in October 1997 but were not able to exceed fifty-three votes for cloture. Several months later, on February 26, another cloture vote failed by a vote of 51–48. Later in 1998, on September 10, in the wake of the House passage of Shays-Meehan, McCain and Feingold tried one more time but were turned back by a vote of 52–48 for cloture, eight short of the necessary sixty votes.

Campaign Finance Reform and Presidential Politics: 106th Congress, 1999–2000

The progress of reform was slowed during the 106th Congress by the prospect of the upcoming presidential election. Both parties were willing to wait to see whether they would elect the new president and thereby gain some advantage in crafting changes in the campaign finance system.

Despite little prospect in the Senate for breaking the filibuster, Shays and Meehan pushed forward with their legislation in the House. After working unsuccessfully to get the leadership to bring up their bill early in the year, the reformers were given their opportunity in the fall of 1999. This time, the leadership again set up obstacles, but House consideration of the bill was more expeditious than the prolonged debate a year earlier.

In a foreshortened version of the marathon battle in 1998, the House voted down a series of amendments to the Shays-Meehan bill. The House passed H.R. 417, the Bipartisan Campaign Finance Reform Act, by a vote of 252 to 177 on September 14, 1999.

With little doubt about the outcome, the Senate again turned back an effort to end a filibuster by a vote of 52–48 on October 19, 1999.

However, McCain and Feingold were by now nationally recognized reform leaders who were becoming more intense in their pursuit of change in Congress. In 1998, Feingold had publicly demanded that the Democratic party and labor unions stop spending soft money for campaign ads thinly disguised as issue education. Wisconsin was the unwilling pioneer of this type of campaign spending, making Feingold and other Wisconsin politicians acutely aware of the problem. McCain was launching a presidential campaign that would generate excitement around an issue that had never been salient for politicians, that is, an issue that won or lost campaigns. Along with Democratic senator and presidential candidate Bill Bradley (D-N.J.), McCain made campaign finance reform central to their candidacies. In the 2000 election, five Senate opponents of campaign finance reform would lose and be replaced by candidates supporting reform.

Conclusion

We do not know (in late March 2001) the outcome of the McCain-Feingold/ Shays-Meehan effort this year, but there is a treacherous obstacle course ahead even if McCain and Feingold succeed in the Senate. Whatever the outcome, reformers will be faced with difficult decisions. If a real reform bill is enacted, what is the next step, and how can the momentum be sustained for further reforms that will surely become necessary? If reform stalls again in Congress, will it be possible to regain the momentum that seemed so powerful during the 2000 election? Will 2001 mark the end of this cycle of reform, or the start of a new cycle?

Notes

1. Dionne, E. J. "Op-ed." *Washington Post,* Mar. 20, 2001.

2. In the Senate, if a senator or group of senators chooses, they can "filibuster." Traditionally, this has meant speaking uninterrupted for hours or days, but Senate rules were changed so that senators can essentially declare a filibuster but not be required to actually speak.

3. Although the cycle described in this article began in the Senate in 1985, the Boren-Goldwater PAC limit bill had a precursor in the House in 1979. Representatives David Obey (D-Wis.) and Tom Railsback (R-Ill.) introduced a bill, H.R. 4970, the Campaign Contribution Reform Act, that was defeated by a vote of 217–198 on October 17, 1979. The bill included a $70,000 aggregate PAC limit for House candidates. The bill was not considered in the Senate. Obey, joined by Rep. Mike Synar (D-Okla.) and Rep. James Leach (R-Iowa), continued this effort over the next two congresses but failed to get the bill out of committee. As noted, there were no significant votes on campaign finance reform during the 97th and 98th congresses.

4. To end a filibuster, sixty senators must vote to "invoke cloture." Thus on any issue that is at all controversial, a majority does not suffice; instead, three-fifths of the Senate is required.

5. *Congressional Quarterly Almanac,* 1992, p. 65.

6. *Congressional Quarterly Almanac,* 1993, pp. 3-5.

7. *Paycheck protection* refers to changes in labor law that require labor unions to exact written permission from union members before any union dues money is spent on political activity.

8. *Congressional Quarterly Almanac,* 1998, p. 18.

Scott Harshbarger is president and CEO of Common Cause and former Attorney General of Massachusetts.

Edwin Davis is Common Cause's national director of state organizations and field operations.

Localism and Reform:
The Benefits of Political Diversity

Carl Castillo, Mike McGrath

One result of last year's presidential election is heightened interest in voting systems and political reform. Media coverage of the tight race between Al Gore and George W. Bush publicized weaknesses in American election practices: confusing ballots, outmoded voting equipment, and poorly funded election offices. As Scott Harshbarger of Common Cause said in a statement posted on the Common Cause Website shortly after the election, "Our newfound awareness of the fragility of the election process should help us tackle these challenges and make our democracy stronger and more vibrant."

The election controversy spawned a range of reform proposals, everything from abolishing the electoral college to implementing a uniform election system throughout the country. In fact, a poll taken by the *Washington Post* shortly after the 2000 election found that a majority of Americans wanted to "strip authority for setting election rules from local and state officials" and give it to the federal government. Nationalizing the electoral process, however, would be a major departure from our country's tradition of localism and respect for state's rights. As tempting as a one-size-fits-all solution may be, experience suggests that in politics, as in nature, a certain level of diversity is a critical element of renewal.

Although the national media often focus on what is happening (or not happening) in Washington, there is much more innovation and experimentation occurring in faraway places such as Westminster, Colorado; or Portland, Maine. Before anyone had ever heard of a hanging chad or butterfly ballot, states were already experimenting with new methods of voting. Last year, Arizona's Democratic party held the country's first binding presidential primary election using the Internet. The result: a whopping 600 percent increase in voter turnout. Oregon is the first state to rely exclusively on mail-in ballots for general elections, a practice that has increased turnout by about 10 percent.

Other jurisdictions are experimenting with instant runoff voting (IRV), a practice that would prevent the "spoiler" problem most recently associated with Ralph Nader's 2000 campaign. With IRV, voters are allowed to choose their candidates in order of preference. If no candidate receives a majority after the first tally, the candidate with the fewest first place votes is eliminated. Ballots cast for that candidate then go to one of the remaining candidates, according to the voters' second choices. The process is repeated until one candidate wins a majority. Several states—Alaska, California, Maryland, New Mexico, Vermont, and Washington—are currently considering IRV legislation, a practice that has already been adopted in Vancouver, Washington; as well as in San Leandro, Oakland, and Santa Clara County, California.

The truth is that Washington seems to have become the last place to look in seeking political innovation. Consider the fate of campaign finance reform. The explosion of soft-money expenditures in national elections was evident in the early 1990s. It has taken Congress all of ten years to consider a remedy to the soft-money problem. At the same time, state and local jurisdictions have been innovating freely, passing and fine-tuning public finance systems, contribution limits, conflict of interest laws, time limits for fundraising, and systems for publicizing candidate compliance with voluntary spending limits. To paraphrase author David Osborne, these state and local jurisdictions have become the true "laboratories of democracy."

Experiments in Campaign Finance Reform

The response by local government to the issue of money in politics is a classic example of the benefit of recognizing and promoting local reform efforts. Recognizing the need for reformers to learn from each other's successes and failures in this particular area, the National Civic League began systematically tracking local campaign finance efforts. In the summer of 1998, with generous funding from the Ford Foundation, this research led to publication of "Local Campaign Finance Reform: Case Studies, Innovations, and Model Legislation." The report detailed seventy-five municipalities that had passed legislation limiting contribution limits to, and expenditures by, candidates for local office. Since that time, forty additional cities have been identified. The approaches used in these cities vary significantly. An overall message emerges from the examples of the approaches detailed here: local experimentation not only allows custom-tailored reforms and overall citizen empowerment but also creates diverse examples that are essential to the continuing evolution of democratic practices.

The Range of Choices. One of the most daunting challenges for political reformers is the impact of court rulings. For those involved in campaign finance reform, the 1976 Supreme Court decision in *Buckley v. Valeo* is the essential reference point for all legislation. In that case, the Supreme Court held that mandatory limits on campaign spending were a violation of the free speech protections afforded by the First Amendment. With this decision, one of the most intuitive solutions to decreasing the role of money in politics was effectively removed as an option. Nevertheless, dozens of cities and counties responded to the challenge by creatively seeking ways of accomplishing the same goal through alternative means.

Table 1. Summary of Contributions to City Council Candidates Exceeding $100 in Boulder, Colorado, Elections 1993–1999

Summary by Year	All Candidates (Percent)	Winning Candidates Only (Percent)
1993	3.9	2.2
1995	12.9	10.4
1997	8.7	5.3
1999	2	0

Voluntary Spending Limits: Boulder, Colorado. Following the lead of Chapel Hill, North Carolina, citizens in the city of Boulder, Colorado, chose to adopt a program of voluntary spending limits that relied on nothing more than the pressure of media publicity as the incentive for candidates to comply. A college town with a long tradition of grassroots politics, Boulder experienced a sharp increase in campaign spending in 1995. Along with the higher sums came paid political consultants, "push polls," and paid "volunteers" in local campaigns. One council candidate spent four times the average amount raised by previous winners. Local political reformers organized a series of meetings to seek input from a broad spectrum of local citizens. The result was a voluntary program modeled after one that had been tried just two years earlier in Chapel Hill. The citizen-run program called on city council candidates to sign a pledge to limit spending to $11,000, to refuse contributions larger than $100, and to give no more than $2,500 in personal funding to their own campaigns. The coalition monitored candidate spending and publicized the results of the program. Benefiting from significant coverage by the local media, the program was considered a success in the 1997 and 1999 election cycles in which it was used. Indeed, by 1999, all but one candidate abided by the spending limits, and all candidates elected were pledge signers (see Table 1).

After the success in 1997, supporters of the program immediately set about promoting a ballot initiative to create a partial public financing system that included mandatory contribution limits and voluntary spending limits for those who accepted matching funds. The public financing initiative passed in 1999 with 62.5 percent of the vote. Supporters of the measure considered the awareness created by the voluntary program as a main reason for its success.

Conflict of Interest: Westminster, Colorado. Another Colorado community discovered a clever way of addressing the campaign finance conundrum through conflict-of-interest laws. In 1996, the city of Westminster amended its charter to apply existing conflict-of-interest regulations to city council campaigns. Under the change, any candidate who accepts more than $100 from a contributor is considered to have a conflict of interest in any official action that uniquely benefits that contributor and therefore must abstain from debating or voting on such action. The amendment seems to have had an effect on campaign contributions. After the amendment, the number of contributions exceeding $100 dropped from thirty-three in 1995 to only fifteen in 1997. One advantage of the conflict-of-interest approach is that it imposes a lesser restriction on free speech rights than does a direct cap on contributions. Ironically, it does not prevent contributors from giving money. Instead, it simply makes the contributors aware that the candidate whom they give to may not be able to vote on an issue of vital concern to them. Another advantage is that conflict-of-interest laws exist in many jurisdictions. Consequently, this approach can be considered an extension of existing rules preventing elected officials from acting on matters in which they have a direct personal interest.

Contribution Limits

The most common reform at the local level is the basic contribution limit. The ruling in the *Buckley* v. *Valeo* case allowed limits on contributions as a means of discouraging corruption. Not that the ruling protected contribution limits from court scrutiny. In 1998, for example, a U.S. Court of Appeals ruled against an Arkansas law that limited contributions to candidates to $100. Judge Arnold Morris wrote that the limits "were too low to allow meaningful participation in protected speech and association."

In January 2000, however, the U.S. Supreme Court upheld a Missouri law limiting contributions for statewide offices to $1,075. Proponents of campaign finance reform considered the *Nixon* v. *Shrink Missouri Government PAC* ruling an important victory. The Court ruled that a state did not need hard evidence of political corruption to justify limits. It also allowed flexibility in setting contribution limits, stating that the limits were permissible unless they were "so radical in effect as to render political association ineffective, drive the sound of a candidate's voice below the level of notice, and render contributions pointless."

Proponents of contribution limits say they prevent special-interest groups from dominating an election with large contributions. There is some evidence that contribution limits also depress the general level of spending, thus making a campaign more affordable. After the District of Columbia imposed $100 limits on its 1994 municipal elections, a study from the Center for New Democracy showed that the total value of contributions dropped by one-fourth. After a 1995 Cincinnati law limiting campaign contributions was overturned by the city council, campaign spending increased dramatically during the 1999 council races.

But contribution limits may have unforeseen consequences. Some critics suggest that contribution limits lead to greater activity by independent expenditure committees that contribute money to support or oppose a candidate without being officially associated with the candidate's committee. Such contributions are often exempt from local campaign finance limits and not visible to the public. Others suggest that contribution limits make it difficult for a first-time or unknown candidate to raise money and get the message out. Some grassroots and minority candidates have benefited from the generosity of large individual contributions.

Austin, Texas. In November 1997, voters in Austin, Texas, passed a city charter amendment imposing a $100 cap on contributions from individuals and political action committees. The amendment also limited contributions from non-Austin residents to $15,000 and imposed a time restriction on fundraising: "Any candidate for Mayor or City Council, and his or her committee, shall neither solicit nor accept contributions except during the last one hundred eighty days preceding a scheduled election for the office sought or in which the council-member faces recall," according to the amendment.

A distinctive feature of Austin's campaign climate is that the city council does not have district elections. The all-at-large system means that each council member must run citywide, increasing the cost of individual elections substantially. In a large city such as Austin, this can lead to an expensive campaign. During the effort to pass the amendment, City Councilman Gus Garcia supported the idea of district elections as the best way to lower campaign costs. The $100 contribution limit, he said, was "unrealistic."

There have been two elections since the amendment was passed. The results have not been conclusive, but it is clear that within the political community—even among some reformers—there is dissatisfaction with the $100 limit. Some Austin political activists refer to the amendment as the Incumbent Re-Election Act, suggesting that the $100 limit makes it difficult for a challenger to raise enough money for a competitive campaign. One of the original supporters of the amendment, Linda Curtis, ran unsuccessfully for city council in the last election. She now considers the $100 limit "too restrictive." During the 2000 election, voter turnout was lower than in earlier elections, leading some in the media to speculate that the contribution limits may have discouraged participation by making it difficult for a candidate to raise money to pay for mailing and television time.

Ironically, one reformer in Austin sees a benefit in the unpopularity of the system. "The bottom line," said this observer, "is that the business community hates the $100 limits, the city council hates the $100 limits, the mayor hates the $100 limits, the city bureaucracy hates the limits, the political consultants hate them, and the public isn't very well informed. We are actually in a good position. If we don't change the system, we have something the establishment hates. If they sit on their hands (and don't enact more systematic reforms), they're stuck with something they hate."

Supporters of contribution limits suggest that adopting a comprehensive public financing system would make the limits palatable to grassroots candidates. Although Austin has had a limited public financing system since 1996, it only applies to candidates who make it into the runoff. At the time that this article was submitted, a reform group was circulating a petition for an initiative to adopt a public financing system for primary races and runoffs. If adopted, the new law would increase the contribution limit to $200 per contributor.

San Francisco. San Francisco's twenty-year-old campaign finance ordinance limited contributions to a candidate to $500. The San Francisco City Attorney interpreted the ordinance to mean that the $500 limit also applied to contributions to independent expenditure committees and political action committees supporting or opposing a candidate. The ordinance also included a provision for voluntary spending limits. Candidates who did not observe the voluntary limits were limited to $150 per contributor.

In May 1999, a group called San Franciscans for Sensible Government (SFSG) filed suit against the city to remove the contribution limit on independent expenditure committees. The group had opposed San Francisco supervisorial candidate Tom Ammiano in a 1998 election. In the suit, the group contended, "as a result of the limits imposed by the ordinance, and the San Francisco City Attorney's interpretation of the ordinance, SFSG PAC's ability to communicate with voters about Supervisor Ammiano's record was significantly hindered." U.S. District Judge Claudia Wilkins issued an injunction, and the city settled out of court, agreeing not to enforce the limit on contributions to independent expenditure committees. Another litigant challenged the variable limit on contributions to a candidate who did not agree to voluntary spending limits. Again, the court issued an injunction and the city settled, agreeing not to enforce the variable limit.

As a result of the settlements, candidates were left with no incentive to stay within the voluntary spending limits, and PACs and independent expenditure committees were left without any contribution limits. Consequently, independent expenditures exploded, going from a mere $13,000 in the 1995 mayoral race to $3.2 million in 1999. The lion's share of that amount was contributed to the winning candidate.

Prodded by Common Cause, the Sierra Club, the League of Women Voters, and Supervisor Ammiano, the San Francisco Ethics Commission drafted the Fair Elections Ordinance, which was placed on the November 2000 ballot. The measure, which included new contribution limits and a public financing system, passed with 52 percent of the vote. The new law maintains the existing limits on contributions to a candidate's committee at $500 in a general election and $250 in a runoff. In addition, it imposes explicit limits on contributions to PACs and independent expenditure committees that are more generous than before. Groups and individuals may spend up to $500 per committee, but they are able to spend $3,000 per calendar year if they contribute to six committees. It is thought that the more generous aggregate limit will discourage legal action.

Public Financing

Like Austin and San Francisco, more and more states and local governments throughout the country are turning to publicly financed elections as a way of limiting campaign spending without running afoul of *Buckley v. Valeo*. The specifics of a public financing system can vary substantially. Eligibility to receive funding generally requires demonstrating a threshold level of support from constituents. This support can be shown through collecting a set number of signatures or by receiving several small contributions. Once a candidate is qualified, public financing is generally provided in one of five ways: (1) matching grants for contributions received, (2) partial or "block" grants, (3) full public financing, (4) free or reduced-rate radio or television time, or (5) a combination of all of these. The conditions for receiving these funds may also include mandatory participation by candidates in a set number of debates.

Currently, there are at least twelve local governments that have a system in place for publicly financed campaigns. They include small cities (such as Boulder, Colorado; and Cary, North Carolina) as well as large ones (New York, Los Angeles). Of these, at least five have had actual experience using their system. All of the cities have seen a level of success sufficient to justify retaining the general model of matching funds, albeit with some refinements and enhancements. New York is an example. New York's Campaign Finance Board has a mandate to review the strengths and limitations of its campaign finance system after each election and recommend change as necessary. In 1998, after a decade of experience with reformed elections, and as a result of one such series of recommendations, New York's City Council enacted several changes to its campaign finance law. Most notable was a change in the matching-funds ratio from 1:1 to 4:1 (four dollars of public money for every dollar of private funds raised in contributions of up to $250). Nicole Gordon, executive director of the Campaign Finance Board, says that the city made this change after recognizing that "high-end contributions were still having an extremely big impact on campaigns." The change in the matching-funds ratio was made to increase the incentive for city residents to make even small contributions.

In 1990, the citizens of Los Angeles adopted a comprehensive system of partial public financing. Administered by the city's Ethics Commission, the public financing program in Los Angeles was first put to the test in 1993. Eight years later, the city's 3.6 million residents are now experiencing their fifth reformed election season.

To qualify for public funding in Los Angeles, a candidate for local office must first be opposed by another viable candidate running for the same office. The candidate must then demonstrate a threshold level of support by raising $25,000 for the city council race, or $150,000 for the mayoral race, from sources other than the candidate or his or her immediate family. Contributions to both participating and nonparticipating candidates may not exceed a $500 limit for the city council race and a $1,000 limit for the mayoral race.

Along with demonstrating a threshold level of support, the participating candidate must agree to limit overall and personal spending on the campaign. In the primary, a candidate for city council agrees to spend no more than $25,000 of personal funds and $330,000 overall; a candidate for mayor agrees not to spend more than $100,000 of personal funds and $2.2 million overall. For the general election, a candidate for city council agrees not to spend more than $25,000 of personal funds and $275,000 overall, and for mayoral candidates the agreed limits are no more than $100,000 of personal funds and no more than $1.76 million overall. Finally, participating candidates agree to debate their opponents at least once in the primary and twice in the general election.

In return for these self-imposed limitations, participating candidates become eligible to receive one dollar in public funds for every dollar they raise, with these qualifications:

- Only the first $500 of each contribution in the case of a candidate for mayor, city attorney, or controller, and the first $250 in the case of a candidate for city council, can be matched.
- Only contributions received within a year of the election are matched.
- Only contributions from individuals are matched. Corporations, unions, political action committees, businesses, or other organizations are not considered to be individuals.
- The maximum amount of matching funds to participating candidate is $100,000 for a council candidate and $667,000 for a mayoral candidate in the primary, and $125,00 for council and $800,000 for mayor in the general election.

The Los Angeles system also addresses independent expenditures. The Ethics Commission regulates the impact of these expenditures in three ways. First, it limits to $500 per person per calendar year the amount that may be contributed to any committee that makes independent expenditures to support or oppose a city candidate or candidates. Second, reporting is required by any person who makes an independent expenditure totaling $1,000 or more. Third, matching-fund candidates are no longer bound by the agreed-upon spending limits once independent expenditures made in support of, or in opposition to, any candidate in a particular race exceed $50,000 for the council race or $200,000 for the mayoral race.

Although L.A.'s comprehensive campaign finance program has been in effect for only four complete elections, some preliminary observations can be made:

- The funding source has proven itself adequate and reliable.
- The level of candidate participation is quite high.
- A majority of races are being won by matching-fund participants.
- Average candidate expenditure levels have remained relatively stable.
- The gap between the amount raised by incumbents and challengers has been reduced, possibly helping to make races more competitive.
- The candidates report spending less time fundraising and more time discussing the issues.
- The number of individual contributions to participating candidates is greater than it is for nonparticipants.
- Independent expenditures are on the increase.

Unlike the unlimited campaign spending that continues to plague other levels of government, spending by candidates for city office has been kept relatively stable. In all but one election since the reform was enacted, the amount spent was actually less than the levels spent in the election immediately preceding the reforms. Although incumbents continue to outpace challengers in fundraising, the gap is narrowing. In the elections prior to the matching-fund program, incumbents held a significant advantage over challengers. For example, one month before the election, their advantage was measured by a twelve-to-one margin. After the reforms were put in place, the margin decreased to less than five-to-one a month before the election. This change is due to a combination of the city's matching-fund program and its prohibition of nonelection year fundraising. The effect is to level the playing field and create the possibility of more competitive elections. According to Rebecca Avila, former executive director of the Los Angeles Ethics Commission, "it's important to note that the gap between challenger and incumbent fundraising is only narrowed when you have challengers who are viable and qualified to receive matching funds. This program does not create viable candidates. It helps viable candidates get their message out."

Public Financing in the States

At least twenty-eight states have some form of public financing. As of 1996, Maine, Massachusetts, and Arizona had all authorized the full voluntary public financing system known as Clean Money/Clean Elections; and Vermont had passed a variation of this same system. Although particular provisions vary with the jurisdiction, under a Clean-Money/Clean-Election system a candidate receives full public financing for the campaign in exchange for forgoing private campaign contributions. The candidate is required to demonstrate a threshold level of popular support to qualify; in some instances there may be a debate requirement and a provision for reduced-cost access to broadcast media as well.

In the 2000 election cycle, Maine, Arizona, and Vermont all held elections for the first time under the new system. Preliminary review of these states shows that Clean-Money laws have led to greater voter choice, an increase in the number of contested races, and more grassroots campaigning. According to Nick Nyhart, executive director of Public Campaign, "Clean Money does what our current campaign finance system fails to do. It allows people to run based on their qualifications and abilities and not the size of their campaign coffers. Candidates campaign on a level playing field, putting their time into voters and issues, instead of the special interest money chase."

With the availability of public funding, the number of viable candidates running for office appears to be on the rise. Maine witnessed a 40 percent increase in the number of contested primaries; the number of people running for office in Arizona increased by 59 percent. In Vermont, there was greater competition in the gubernatorial race with the emergence of Progressive Party candidate Anthony Pollina. His campaign might have garnered little attention had he depended on private funding. According to Northeast Action, a regional organization working on the issue, public funding boosted his candidacy by giving him the resources to compete and ensured that his campaign was taken seriously by the process.

Further evidence of the effectiveness of the Clean-Money/Clean-Election systems was visible in candidate participation. In Maine, 116 of 352 legislative candidates opted into the system; 32 percent were incumbents. Clean-Money candidates also demonstrated their ability to win. In Arizona, 36 percent of Clean-Money candidates won, and in Maine, even when opposed by privately financed candidates, 53 percent of Clean-Money candidates were victorious.

Lessons Learned

With nearly three decades of experimentation in campaign finance reform at the state and local levels, certain lessons are apparent. For one thing, we've learned that, as with most types of reform, campaign finance reform must always be tailored to the size and character of the community. Although a voluntary system of contribution and spending limits may be effective in the small town of Alta, Utah, such a system may be completely unrealistic in a large city such as Philadelphia. Second, we've seen that more and more, cities, counties, and states are recognizing the importance of publicly financed elections and are moving in that direction. Even within public financing, the tendency seems to be to move from less financial support to more, from partial to full public financing.

We've also seen that these changes are often incremental. Citizens in Vermont supported a full public financing system paid for by general tax revenues only after they saw the shortcomings of partial public financing supported by a voluntary tax checkoff system. This movement toward public financing is currently the trend, but a change in federal regulation of the media or a pivotal decision from the Supreme Court could quickly bring a new approach into fashion. Finally, we've seen the importance of continually reviewing and reevaluating the effectiveness of a program after each election. If the goal is to limit the influence of money, new loopholes can and will always be found. Without continual review of the administration, regulation, and laws of the program, the goals are quickly subverted.

Conclusion

In this article, we have focused on diverse approaches to campaign finance reform at the state and local levels and how innovation is flourishing throughout the country. We have little doubt that a similarly wide range of approaches can be found in other efforts to renew our democratic institutions—election system reform, technological improvements, civic participation models, and basic forms of representation. Not all of these efforts are likely to be successful. But a community learns what works by experimentation, and it is likely to continue to evolve and adapt its chosen reforms to fit the political environment. Although last year's confusion over ballots and voting machines reminds us of the need for uniformity and standards when it comes to basic principles of fairness and equal representation, the advantage of allowing diversity in developing reform models has been clearly established by the communities we have observed. These communities are laboratories for experimentation and change.

When we think about the complexity of political reform, we are tempted to use a biological analogy. The search for effective political system reform requires a large "gene pool" of states and municipalities. Despite a climate that is often hostile to change, state and local reformers are constantly testing new ideas, adapting their practices, and affording new case studies for future reference. This diversity should be nourished and celebrated. Whenever we imagine that we have an answer that can work for every community, we should consider the possible cost to our future ability to adapt and evolve.

Carl Castillo is the director of the New Politics Program of the National Civic League.

Mike McGrath is a senior policy analyst with the New Politics Program.

New York City's Campaign Finance System: Why Is the Best Hope for Reform Being Ignored?

Mark Schmitt

The movement for campaign finance reform, although it is finally beginning to show progress, has recently diverged along two branches, leaving a vast unexplored territory between them. Some of the most promising ideas for reducing the influence of money on democracy may be found in that middle ground.

One branch, following Senators McCain and Feingold, pursues incremental reform at the federal level, aiming to close the loopholes—most notably, soft-money funding of political parties—that have allowed the corrupting power of huge donations to reenter political campaigns.

The other branch disdains such incrementalism and the compromise of congressional politics. It considers big soft-money contributions no worse than regulated hard money. This branch of reformers starts from the premise that all private funding of political campaigns is corrupting because it magnifies the very inequalities of wealth that democracy ought to ameliorate. The preferred solution for this school—the only plausible solution when the problem is stated in this way—is full public financing of all campaigns.

These two alternatives have received the lion's share of public attention and enthusiasm. Federal legislation, in the form of the McCain-Feingold bill, has been the main focus of media attention, and its Senate passage was the most closely watched congressional drama since the Clinton impeachment melodrama. Passage was far from a guarantee that the soft-money ban will become law; nonetheless, it demonstrated that campaign finance reform had become, at last, a winning issue.

At the state level, however, and among grassroots activists, it is the more sweeping approach, Clean Money, that has generated the most enthusiasm (see the article by Castillo and McGrath in this issue of the *National Civic Review*). Under this model of full public financing, candidates for office are given the option of renouncing virtually all private funding in exchange for a fixed grant of enough money to run a typical campaign for that office. Over the last four years, voters in Maine, Massachusetts, and Arizona bypassed their legislatures to enact full public financing by ballot initiative. In Maine, the system took effect in 2000, and more than one-third of candidates for the legislature chose to renounce all private money to run under the system. Arizona and Massachusetts are preparing to implement the program this year.

Washington has begun to take note of the public interest in full public financing. *Washington Post* columnist David Broder wrote favorably about it after meeting a number of the enthusiastic candidates from Maine, including conservative Republicans as well as liberal Democrats. An amendment to allow states to implement Clean-Money reform for congressional campaigns was the only alternative approach to campaign finance reform considered during the Senate debate on McCain-Feingold, winning thirty-six votes.

There is a third option for reform, however, one that has been entirely overlooked by the media and reform activists. Partial public financing, either through a system of matching private contributions with public money or through tax credits to encourage small contributions, is the "Third Way" of campaign finance reform—neither as modest and incremental as the congressional approach nor as grand in its ambitions as the Clean-Money approach. Partial public financing, where it is generous and well designed, shows great promise, not only in political Arcadias such as Maine but also in New York City, where the corruption of politics by money dates back at least to Tammany Hall. It should not be overlooked.

New York City's public financing system has been in place for a decade, but only in 1998 did the city council establish its current form: a public match of four dollars for every dollar raised in contributions of $250 or less from city residents. To qualify for this extraordinary benefit, a candidate must agree to spending limits, which are relatively generous (about $5 million for the mayor's race). However, a candidate who takes maximum advantage of the system would receive more than 60 percent of this amount in public funds.

The system will receive its fullest test in November 2001, when every citywide office and a majority of seats on the city council change hands because of term limits. In special elections for city council seats held since 1998, most races had four or more candidates, and the average contribution was only $135.

For 2001, one thing is already known: of the dozen or so potential candidates for citywide office, all but one (billionaire Republican potential candidate Michael Bloomberg) will participate in the system. They will agree to spending limits, seek to raise as much as possible in small contributions rather than large, and be assured of reasonable parity in their ability to be heard by the voters. That is, no candidate with a reasonable base of popular support has to worry about being completely unable to purchase enough radio or television time, or print enough brochures, to be heard.

New York's system is only one partial-match model that has proven successful. Minnesota's system features a one-to-one match of private contributions, combined with a tax credit (or a cash refund, for those who don't pay taxes) for contributions of $50. As in New York, virtually 100 percent of candidates agree to the spending limits and debates that are conditions of participation in the system.

Partial public financing on this generous model has several distinct advantages as a solution to the problem of money in politics:

- It makes it far easier for candidates who don't have access to wealthy donors to get over the wall that prevents them from being heard by voters.
- It drastically increases the political power of the small contributor, the ordinary citizen who can't imagine giving $1,000 (the current federal limit) but might be able to come up with $250 for a candidate he or she cares passionately about.
- It strongly induces candidates to comply with reasonable spending limits and participate in debates; thus, although not equalizing spending, it brings most viable candidates into the same general range.

Partial public financing is not without drawbacks, especially when compared to full public financing or Clean Money. For one thing, partial public financing does not (and does not try to) eliminate the role of money and fundraising prowess in winnowing the field of candidates. The flagship example of partial public financing, the presidential primary system, seems no healthier than any other aspect of the political process. Although most presidential races begin with a large field of candidates, many (as happened to Republican Elizabeth Dole in 2000) are forced out early because of a lack of money.

But the New York City and Minnesota systems are an evolutionary leap beyond the decades-old presidential matching system. Both give candidates with only modest support and little access to wealth a boost into the big leagues, where they can compete on the basis of their ideas, not their ability to dominate fundraising. But there are two unique aspects of these systems that make them worthy of consideration, especially at the current moment.

First, most candidates participate. All systems that ask candidates to comply with spending limits must be voluntary to comply with the Supreme Court's 1976 ruling in *Buckley v. Valeo*. In every system, candidates make a careful strategic calculus about whether it is preferable for them to participate or step outside the system. Because full public financing asks candidates to commit themselves well in advance to giving up all private fundraising and accepting a fixed level of spending, it is risky, especially given uncertainty about whether other candidates will participate. One-third of legislative candidates in Maine participated in 2000, but gubernatorial candidates in both Maine and Vermont who supported the system have nonetheless chosen not to participate in it. If more and more candidates decline to participate, often because they expect that their opponents will not, the system is no better than the status quo.

A system such as New York City's, however, allows candidates to ease in smoothly as they begin to raise money. A candidate who may not be sure how much money she can raise or what her opponents will spend has no reason not to participate. If the race becomes more expensive, she can redouble her outreach to small contributors. Nor does the presence of a single nonparticipating candidate such as Bloomberg deter others from participating. Since a candidate cannot raise more money than Bloomberg anyway, participating in the system is the best way to be heard against his wealth.

Second, we can't close all the loopholes. Both the McCain-Feingold approach to reform and full public financing must eventually face a disconcerting reality: there will remain money and spending in politics that cannot effectively be regulated. We might eliminate party soft money, but will we ever regulate ads sponsored by independent groups that simply mention a candidate, ads that dominate some campaigns? Will we be able to regulate ads and mailings intended to affect the election by shaping the issue agenda, if they might not even mention a candidate?

The congressional approach assumes that we can. So does full public financing. In a system where a candidate must agree to strict limits and to renounce all private spending, a party or independent group that steps in with ads or mailings, outside the purview of the law, has a uniquely powerful voice, being unconstrained while the candidate is handcuffed. In Maine, a candidate targeted by independent expenditures is to be given additional public funds to respond, but this system depends on a state official being given the authority to determine whether an ad or mailing is intended to influence the election or not—often a difficult distinction to make, and one that raises serious constitutional questions. A candidate who expects to be targeted by outside groups is also unlikely to accept the handcuff of fixed financing.

The New York City system, however, can coexist well in an environment of uncontrolled outside funding. The spending limits are high enough that they do not create an incentive to evade them. (In fact, although New York is a hotbed of well-financed groups and politically active individuals, there has been little independent spending.) A candidate who is targeted by outside groups still has the freedom to turn to small donors and appeal for help.

In short, both the congressional approach and the full public financing approach are absolutely dependent on limits. If the limits fail, if outside money reenters politics, these approaches fail. Partial public financing includes limits, but it is not absolutely dependent on them in the same way. The American Civil Liberties Union has for years been calling for a system of public financing that provides "floors without ceilings"—that is, a system that helps candidates be heard without limiting other candidates or outside voices. The floors-without-ceilings approach is utterly impractical. How can taxpayers be expected to consent to put their money into a campaign unless the candidates agree to restrain their spending in return? But the aspiration is good, and the New York City system comes as close as possible: floors with high ceilings.

The choices in campaign finance reform ultimately are not just between competing systems but also between competing goals. For congressional incrementalists, the goal is to limit specific corruption—the kind that inevitably arises when a single donor can take credit for several hundred thousand or a million dollars of support for a campaign. For Clean-Money advocates, the goal is a broader notion of political equality, in which the inequalities of capitalism are totally isolated from the sphere of democracy. For partial public financing, the goal is something different: to make elections more competitive, to restrain the arms race that drives political spending out of control, and to make big donors far less important to a campaign. These are more modest goals, but if they can be achieved, they will go a long way toward reducing money's distortion of the democratic process.

Mark Schmitt is the director of the Program on Governance and Public Policy of the Open Society Institute.

Free Airtime: Another Means for Cleaning Up Campaigns

Matt Farrey

For decades now, the congressional debate about campaign finance has played out along familiar lines. Reformers charge that there's too much money in politics and that new laws are needed to prevent the corrupting influence of unlimited political contributions. Opponents of reform argue it costs money to communicate a political message and that any laws that limit campaign contributions also limit speech. It's time to look at this old conundrum from a new perspective.

Reformers should search for ways to do more than limit the supply of political money; they should also look for ways to promote political speech. Opponents of reform should acknowledge that any campaign finance system that puts a high price tag on political speech runs contrary to the intent of the First Amendment—the very thing they claim to champion. Is there a way out of this box?

The key to comprehensive reform is to restrain the *demand* for political money at the same time as one limits its *supply*—and do so in a way that ensures an open flow of campaign communication. The best place to craft a solution on this front is at the greatest source of the problem: broadcast television. It is both the most widely used medium for political communication and the driving force behind the high cost of politics. In nearly every other country, broadcasters are required as a condition of receiving their licenses to provide free airtime to candidates and parties during the height of the campaign season. In this country, broadcasters have increasingly come to view political campaigns as an opportunity to profiteer rather than to inform—and they do so using tens of billions of dollars worth of airwaves they have been granted, free of charge, in return for a pledge to serve the public interest. It's time to require that our broadcast industry make good on this commitment by providing free airtime for candidate ads and discourse.

The High Cost of Political Speech

If you want to run for public office, advocate for the candidates and positions of your political party, or educate the public about issues, you need to communicate with voters. Even with the emergence of cable television and the

Internet, broadcast television is still the medium that gives you the largest audience. So if you want to be a player in the political process, you have to get on TV. Broadcast television should be the heart and soul of a system of political communication that encourages a wide-open, dynamic debate about candidates and issues.

But most broadcasters don't see it that way. The media corporations that own the major networks and the nation's thirteen hundred local commercial TV stations pressure station managers to achieve huge profits and put the interests of democracy on the back burner. They view politics as a ratings loser; as a result, they give scant coverage to candidates and issues during the campaign season. This forces candidates, parties, and issue groups who want to be on broadcast television—and they all do—to pay their way on, thirty seconds at a time. In the 2000 election, this "pay to play" model of political communication sent the cost of politics to an unprecedented level.

Analysis of advertising sales in the 75 largest television markets in the country found that candidates, parties, and interest groups spent $771 million on political advertising in 2000.[1] If we add in estimates from the more than 130 smaller media markets in the country, it is reasonable to conclude that as much as $1 billion was spent on political advertising last year. This is a fivefold increase over what political advertisers spent on broadcast television ads in 1980, even after adjusting for inflation. One reason for this explosion in spending is that the political parties have discovered and exploited loopholes in the campaign finance laws that allow them to raise unlimited contributions from wealthy individuals, corporations and unions—the so-called soft money.

The Annenberg Public Policy Center (APPC) estimates that the Democratic and Republican parties spent a combined total of more than $162 million to buy advertising time just in the period from Super Tuesday (March 7) through Election Day. At the same time, issue groups also scrambled to get airtime to run ads on their issues. APPC estimates that while parties and candidates were spending heavily to communicate with voters, issue groups spent approximately $345 million to get out their own message. Analysis of party and issue ad spending in the top seventy-five markets found that the two major political parties and nine interest groups accounted for 90 percent of the issue ad spending in the top markets. The top spender was Citizens for Better Medicare, funded by the health care industry, which spent $25.4 million. Second was the AFL-CIO, with a total of $9.5 million.[2] These figures demonstrate the consequences of the pay-to-play system of political communication. Only those candidates, parties, and groups that are capable of raising millions of dollars are able to have a voice in the debate.

Another consequence of this scramble to buy television time during elections is the inflationary effect it has on the cost of advertising for political candidates. In 1971, Congress instituted a lowest unit charge (LUC) system for political advertising by candidates. The intent was to guarantee that candidates would not be charged more than a television station's most-favored product advertiser. With this law, Congress was recognizing the value of political speech and attempting to insulate it, but not completely remove it, from the pressures of the free market.

But according to analysis by ten local stations in large markets during the 2000 election, this LUC system has completely broken down and no longer serves the purpose for which it was designed. The study, conducted by the Alliance for Better Campaigns, found that on average candidates buying time on those ten stations paid a rate that was 65 percent higher than the lowest candidate rate listed on the stations' advertising rate cards.[3] The reason? Station sales managers have managed to find ways to avoid the intent of the LUC system while not violating the actual letter of the law. They have developed a complex rate system that establishes "classes" of time for advertising. Typically, candidates can get the lowest unit rate only for ad time that is "preemptible." If a station sells an ad to a candidate and then gets a better offer from another advertiser, it can bump the candidate from that time and sell it to the higher bidder. In the midst of the thrust and parry of a political campaign, candidates need to get their message out as quickly as possible. If their ads are constantly being bumped by other advertisers, they lose the battle of political persuasion. So most candidates opt to pay the higher, nonpreemptible rate that guarantees their ad will run.

Stations are also allowed to change their ad rates weekly or even daily, depending upon demand. In the crunch time during the weeks leading up to an election, stations tend to raise all of their rates—preemptible, nonpreemptible, and all the gradations in between. Political ad buyers report being quoted one rate for an ad in the morning and a higher rate for the same ad later the same day. Some issue groups (which are not entitled to LUC protection) saw their ad rates double and even triple between Labor Day and Election Day. As the rates for issue groups rose, those charged to candidates drifted up with them.

The McCain-Feingold bill, passed by the U.S. Senate in April 2001, included a provision to address the price-gouging problem. Senators Robert Torricelli (D-N.J.), Richard Durbin (D-Ill.), John Corzine (D-N.J.), and Byron Dorgan (D-N. Dak.) drafted an amendment that requires broadcasters to offer candidates and political parties an ad rate that is no higher than the lowest rate that the same ad time sold for during the previous 365 days. The amendment also prohibits broadcasters from preempting candidate and party ads if another advertiser is willing to pay a higher rate for the same ad time. Finally, it requires the FCC to conduct random audits during a campaign to ensure that broadcasters are complying with the law. Extending the LUC provision to political parties and eliminating the preemptible class of time for candidate and party ads significantly reduces the cost of political speech. Candidates and parties would not be forced to buy the more expensive, nonpreemptible time. The lowest-unit-rate provisions might begin to serve the purpose for which they were originally enacted.

The Torricelli-Durbin amendment is a step in the right direction because it reduces the cost of political speech for candidates and parties. But broadcasters are likely to find a way around these provisions, just as they did with the original lowest-unit-rate regulations. The amendment is an effective short-term solution. But in the long run, the high cost of political speech requires ambitious and sweeping changes in the structure of political advertising on television.

Broadcasters and the Public Interest

Unlike publishers of newspapers, magazines, and other communications media, broadcasters have always been public trustees as well as private commercial ventures. They have been given free and exclusive rights to use a scarce public resource—the public airwaves—to make a profit. But they have also agreed to "serve the public interest, convenience, and necessity." This standard was part of the 1934 Communications Act, which distributed analog frequencies at first to radio and eventually to television stations. It was also part of the 1996 Telecommunications Act, which gave existing television license holders double the amount of spectrum space they previously had, to facilitate their transition to digital technology. If Congress had auctioned off the digital spectrum, as it began doing in the early 1990s for other commercial users of the spectrum, it could have generated up to $70 billion for the U.S. Treasury. Television broadcasters got their new airwaves for free.

In the wake of what many regarded as a spectrum giveaway, President Clinton appointed a panel of experts to review and update the matter. In 1998, the panel, known as the Advisory Commission on the Public Interest Obligations of Broadcasters in the Digital Age, made a promising recommendation to deal with political discourse. It called on the national networks and local television stations to voluntarily agree to air a minimum of five minutes per night of "candidate-centered discourse" in the thirty nights prior to all primary and general elections. This "5/30" standard gave the stations the flexibility to make these segments work within the regular flow of their prime time news and public affairs programs; the segments could be in a variety of formats, such as brief debates, interviews, and statements by candidates on important issues. The panel's recommendation called for stations to take action voluntarily without the government forcing them to do it as a condition of their license to operate. This was a compromise between the public interest advocates on the panel, who favored a government mandate, and the broadcasters, who adamantly opposed a mandate of any kind. Because CBS President Leslie Moonves cochaired the panel, there was reason to hope that the industry would embrace this recommendation.

In 1999 and 2000, the Alliance for Better Campaigns waged a national and state-level public education and advocacy campaign designed to encourage station managers to meet this 5/30 standard. Twenty-two national organizations;

twenty-five state groups; and more than two hundred prominent civic, political, academic, and religious leaders signed on as supporters. By October 2000, five station groups (Hearst-Argyle, E.W. Scripps, Capitol Broadcasting, CBS, and NBC, all on behalf of their local stations, but not their networks) had made public commitments to the standard. These five groups own a total of seventy-five local stations. In addition, eighteen other local stations made commitments, bringing the total to ninety-three. Although that figure amounted to just 7 percent of the nation's thirteen hundred local television stations, these ninety-three stations are located in markets that reach more than 60 percent of the television households in the country. In other words, these commitments, though modest, represented a significant opportunity to increase the flow of political speech on television.

As the campaign season played out, however, the television industry fell well short of the 5/30 standard. The APPC found that in the month before the November 7 election, the three major broadcast networks (ABC, CBS, and NBC) devoted an average of just sixty-four seconds per network per night to candidate discourse.[4] Meanwhile, local TV stations across the country devoted an average of seventy-four seconds a night to candidate discourse in the month before November 7, according to the Lear Center at the University of Southern California's survey of local stations in the nation's top fifty-eight media markets. But the Lear survey also showed that stations making a commitment to the 5/30 standard aired three times more candidate-centered discourse than those refusing to make a commitment—two minutes and seventeen seconds per night versus forty-five seconds per night.[5] It also showed that stations that had committed to the 5/30 standard aired a far higher percentage of substantive, issue-based coverage than other stations. So the initial faith in the promise of the standard proved to be well founded. Unfortunately, the vast majority of TV broadcasters chose to ignore it.

Solution: Fewer Dollars, More Speech

What can be done? With a little ingenuity and a lot of political will, we can create a system of political communication that reduces the demand for political money, protects First Amendment values and encourages the open, dynamic, free-wheeling debate that we want in a democracy. To do this, we need to address two problems head on. First, we must reduce the demand for political money by addressing the high cost of political advertising. Second, we must increase the supply of political speech on TV.

Research by the Alliance for Better Campaigns suggests that the LUC system is not an effective way to control costs. Price controls have a poor track record in the free market economy, and the LUC system is no exception. It should be replaced with a system of mandatory free airtime for candidates and political parties. The alliance has proposed creating a "national political broadcast time bank" to distribute vouchers for free advertising time to qualifying candidates and political parties. The broadcast bank would be stocked with a total of $750 million in vouchers beginning in 2002 and then be indexed to rise with inflation in every even-numbered election year thereafter.

Under the proposal, television stations are assessed an annual spectrum usage fee—a tiny percentage of their gross revenues—to underwrite the bank. The Federal Communications Commission distributes $500 million in vouchers to political parties and $250 million to candidates for federal office. To qualify, federal candidates are required to raise a threshold number of small contributions from individuals and agree to overall campaign spending limits.

Free access to advertising time would open up the political process by making it possible for more candidates—including those who are neither wealthy nor well connected to special interests—to wage a competitive campaign for public office. The proposed approach also cleanses and reinvigorates political parties. In modern American politics, the party has become little more than a fundraising operation. The Republican and Democratic parties raised just under $500 million in soft-money contributions in the 1999–2000 campaign. Although soft money is not supposed to be used to "expressly advocate" for the defeat or election of a particular candidate, parties increasingly spend this money on issue ads that avoid express advocacy but are clearly intended to benefit a particular candidate. The parties go through a variety of contortions to avoid the meaningless distinction between "candidate" and "issue" ads. By giving vouchers for free advertising to the political parties, we recognize that parties ought to be in the business of helping their candidates get elected. We also advance the ideal of a vigorous democracy in which election campaigns are a contest of well-identified, well-articulated policies and political philosophies.

Another benefit of giving free ad time to the parties is that it makes more congressional races competitive. Most political money is spent in open-seat races, as well as the handful where a challenger has a credible shot of defeating an incumbent. The vast majority of incumbent members of Congress face no serious opposition. The parties are the only political institution with a vested interest in increasing competition. If the major parties (and qualifying minor parties) have free ad time vouchers, they will be more willing to commit resources in races where they have a credible but underfunded challenger to an incumbent of the other party.

A voucher system for candidates and parties no doubt raises the cost of airtime for other advertisers, including issue groups. One significant development in the last two election cycles is the explosion in spending by "outside" groups such as Citizens for Better Medicare, the AFL-CIO, Planned Parenthood, and the U.S. Chamber of Commerce. These ads are funded by special interests that want to shape public opinion so that candidates who favor their policy positions are elected. In many hotly contested races, these ads dominate the airwaves, reducing the candidates to bit players in their own campaigns. Although the groups have a right to be heard, they have no special right to free advertising time. Candidates are different. After all, they are the ones who stand for public office and, once elected, need to make decisions that are in the public interest.

Opponents of the broadcast-bank proposal usually raise logistical questions. What do we do in large media markets with multiple congressional races? How do we distribute the vouchers fairly? These issues can be addressed by creating a flexible system that imposes an equal and equitable burden on all broadcasters while allowing the political marketplace to allocate the resources efficiently.

Under the voucher proposal, the FCC assesses a spectrum usage fee that is the same percentage of gross advertising revenues (likely to be 1 percent or so) for every station in the country. Broadcasters then redeem the vouchers for money from the broadcast bank. Even if one station in a large media market is flooded with vouchers, the cost to that station does not exceed the 1 percent that it contributed to the bank. Also, the vouchers are designed to be a transferable, flexible resource. Candidates can trade in their vouchers for other resources of equivalent value from the party, such as direct mail or get-out-the-vote drives. It is thus highly unlikely that all of the congressional candidates in the expensive New York media market, for example, will use all of their vouchers. They might prefer a more cost-effective resource such as a phone bank or direct mail. Under a voucher system, they can make such exchanges with their party—which redistributes the airtime vouchers to races where they would do the most good.

The $250 million in vouchers to be distributed to candidates for the Senate and House does not eliminate their need to raise additional funds, but it provides important seed resources that help to level the playing field between incumbents and challengers. Candidates qualify for the vouchers by raising a specified number of small dollar contributions that establish the legitimacy of their candidacy. Typically, there are between eight hundred and one thousand congressional candidates each election year who may qualify for vouchers. Each candidate is eligible for the same amount of vouchers, likely to be $100,000–200,000. Vouchers for Senate candidates are to be distributed on the basis of the voting-age population of the state; $500 million in vouchers are then distributed equally to qualifying political parties. Critics of the McCain-Feingold bill say it starves the political parties, and they have a point. But the response should not be to allow parties to continue to solicit six-figure checks; it should be to give them a clean, abundant resource that they can use to help elect their candidates.

The broadcast-bank proposal significantly reduces the demand for political money, but it still leaves the universe of political communication on television dominated by thirty-second spots. This is a mixed blessing. Scholars continue to debate the merits of political advertising, but most citizens would agree that a thorough, thoughtful public debate cannot be conducted in thirty- and sixty-second ads. Most surveys show that voters are increasingly contemptuous of political advertising, particularly because they are bombarded by it in the weeks before an election.

Citizens need more opportunity to get to know the people who want to represent them and understand their positions on the issues. Broadcasters can give them the opportunity. As a condition of their license, television broadcasters should be required to air a minimum of two hours a week of candidate-centered discourse (debates, interviews, candidate issue statements, and similar formats in the six weeks prior to a general election and two weeks prior to a primary. At least one hour of this total should be aired during prime time so that it reaches the widest possible audience. This proposal is similar in concept to the current "three-hour-rule," which requires broadcasters to provide a minimum of three hours per week of educational programming for children. A few hours for children and a few hours for democracy every couple of years—is that too much to ask for the free grant of billions of dollars worth of public airwaves?

Conclusion

The primary goal of campaign finance reform has been to reduce political corruption by limiting and controlling the supply of political money. These are important ends. Soft money must be banned, and the influence of corporations, unions, and wealthy contributors over elected officials needs to be curbed. But we do a grave disservice to the political process if we ignore the other side of the equation: demand. Currently, huge political contributions are needed to pay for political speech on television. But it does not have to be this way. A system that combines mandatory free airtime for candidates and political parties with a requirement for candidate-centered programming can reduce the cost and increase the supply of political speech on broadcast television. Television can become democracy's "public square," a forum for a thriving, open, and dynamic debate about public issues. Maybe, just maybe, an increasingly cynical and politically disengaged citizenry will start to take a few steps back toward the public square and become active voters.

Notes

1. Alliance for Better Campaigns. "Gouging Democracy: How the Television Industry Profiteered on Campaign 2000." Washington, D.C.: Alliance for Better Campaigns, 2001, p. 3.

2. Annenberg Public Policy Center. "Issue Advertising in the 1999–2000 Election Cycle." Philadelphia: Annenberg Public Policy Center, 2001, p. 3.

3. Alliance for Better Campaigns, 2001, p. 2.

4. Falk, E., and Aday, S. "Are Voluntary Standards Working? Candidate Discourse on Network Evening News Programs." Philadelphia: Annenberg Public Policy Center, 2000, p. 1.

5. Kaplan, M., and Hale, M. "Local TV Coverage of the 2000 General Election." Los Angeles: Annenberg School for Communication, University of Southern California, 2001, p. 1.

Matt Farrey is the associate director of the Alliance for Better Campaigns.

So You Want to Run for President? Ha! Barriers to Third-Party Entry

Ralph Nader, Theresa Amato

Article II of the U.S. Constitution, the part where it says "No person except a natural born citizen, or a citizen of the United States, at the time of the adoption of this Constitution, shall be eligible to the office of President," is disconnected from realpolitik. If it reflected today's reality, it would read more along these lines:

> No person who cannot overcome arcane ballot access laws in fifty states and is not a billionaire shall be eligible to the office of president except those nominated by the reigning duopoly and condoned by the *New York Times* and *Washington Post* or the five polling companies that are contracted to provide polls to the bipartisan, corporate-funded commission on presidential debates lest they be thought to clutter the playing field or deprive one of the other candidates of their rightful entitlement to all the votes that the aspiring person might otherwise take.

Running for president as a third-party candidate permits an eyewitness view of the multifaceted barriers that prevent third parties in this country from competing fairly in the democratic process. The hurdles are so prevalent that leaders of oligarchic regimes in foreign countries might blush. From media coverage to ballot access and participation in the presidential debates, the obstacles to competing in the political process loom large and the political will to reduce them is puny.

Media Coverage

Our campaign was launched in February 2000 to seek the presidential nomination of the Green Party because of the democracy gap in our country. The announcement came at an opening address at the Madison Hotel in Washington, D.C., replete with an extensive explanation about how civil society is having a harder time getting things done because corporate influence and dollars have rendered a bought-and-paid-for political scene in Washington that either is beholden to their corporate paymasters or largely indifferent to corporate control of some of our basic public institutions. The resulting loss attributable to this gap was discussed in detail. The *Washington Post,* which is headquartered across 15th Street, could not be bothered to send a reporter. There were some cameras and other reporters, but almost no coverage. The announcement earned a three-hundred-word squib in the *New York Times,* akin to the amount of space they devote to a couple of marriage notices.

The first lesson of entering the race for president as a citizen seeking a third-party nomination rather than as a major party candidate was that one can count on receiving almost no media coverage. If you don't speak in eight-second sound bites, you're not likely to get coverage in the standard seventeen minutes of corporate news cycles exclusively filled by leads that bleed, lengthy weather reports, cute animal stories, and chitchat between the anchors. Even when the campaign filled Madison Square Garden in mid-October, on ten days' notice, with more than fifteen thousand paying people, the *Washington Post* still did not cover it. The Nader campaign was unique in its ability to draw such large paying crowds to its political rallies. It is one thing to fail to provide daily coverage of third-party candidates, even while routine coverage of major party candidates extends to the trivial, but it is another matter to fail to report the history-making aspects of a third-party campaign.

Throughout the campaign, all that the press wanted to cover was the horse race. A candidate can talk about the death penalty; child poverty; racial profiling; corporate crime, fraud, and abuse; the failed war on drugs; the millions of people without health insurance; campaign finance failures; and all the pressing problems of the day. The candidate can go to all fifty states, to housing projects and homeless shelters, and put out sixty-plus position papers, and two to four press releases a day. Yet at the end of the day, the only thing the press cares about is the horse race and whether a third-party candidate is "stealing" votes from either or both of the major party candidates. The use of the press's language itself is indicative of the two-party mind-set: a candidate who competes in a primary is accorded equal footing as a "challenger" with the "frontrunner," while a third-party candidate who competes in the general election is considered a "spoiler" for daring to enter the duopolists' playing field and stealing votes.

If you do get coverage as a third-party candidate, it is likely to be cast as some kind of style or feature story. Third-party candidates are not news; they are treated just as oddities—or worse, clutter. The *New York Times,* as early as June, pronounced in its lead editorial that the voters should have a clear thumbs up or down choice on just Bush and Gore. The Nader-LaDuke campaign was considered to be cluttering the field. Over the course of the campaign, it became apparent that the *New York Times* would say just about anything to make sure that Al Gore won. This was the case not only for the editorial board, since some reporters would editorialize as well. There were some notable exceptions among the media, such as the *Village Voice* and *The Nation,* but not many.

Of course, most third parties cannot afford much media advertising. Our campaign spent under $2 million on media advertising. Pat Buchanan spent nearly everything from the Reform Party millions on ballot access or advertisements. According to posted FEC records, the Bush campaign spent approximately $73 million on media. The Gore campaign spent approximately $51 million. This does not include what the parties or advocacy groups spent on media on behalf of the major-party candidates. A substantial percentage of the contributions made to campaigns or parties are thus funneled into the television broadcasters' pockets to pay for ads that are mostly displayed in the swing states, with virtually all other states being ignored.

The Alliance for Better Campaigns, a public-interest group led by Paul Taylor, has a study on its Website (www.bettercampaigns.org) about the broadcasters and their price gouging entitled "Gouging Democracy." (See also www.Greedytv.org, and the article in this issue of the *National Civic Review* by Matt Farrey of the alliance.) The television industry raked in more than $770 million for political ads in the 2000 elections; of the stations surveyed, most provided less than forty-five seconds a night of coverage—*total*—for the candidates. No wonder the television networks barely cover the two major party conventions. It appears to be better for their bottom line to freeze out the politicians and make them pay top dollar for ads in order to get any time at all on the publicly owned airwaves.

Of course, since the system serves the duopolists well, neither party in Congress has much incentive to change it. Candidates seem to prefer having controlled messages compacted into thirty-second ads. (Some candidates refused to have a press conference for weeks on end!) If we want fair elections, though, then the landlords of the airwaves—the taxpayers who own this piece of the commonwealth—should be able to require that the tenants (the broadcasters who rent these public assets) provide free airtime to candidates who are on the ballot for public office.

Ballot Access

Apart from the problems in getting coverage, how do candidates for president actually get in the position where the voters can vote for them? In the United States, each state has not only its own specially designed (butterfly) ballot but also its own arcane set of grossly complicated procedures for getting on the ballot. Mind you, bipartisan-controlled state assemblies created all these incredible obstacles.

Richard Winger, who publishes *Ballot Access News* (www.ballot-access.org), does a formidable job of chronicling these outrages. Among the crippling provisions encountered during election 2000, consider these:

- To qualify for the ballot in Texas, a political party needed to collect 37,713 signatures in a seventy-five-day period; those who signed the petition could not have voted in the state's primary.
- In North Carolina, a party needed 51,324 signatures by May 15 of the election year. By statute, the petition has a must-carry phrase that reads "The signers of this petition intend to organize a new political party. . . ." To contemplate the chilling effect, simply ask yourself: When was the last time you signed something that would require you to commit to organizing a new political party?
- In Virginia, a candidate needs 10,000 signatures, four hundred from each congressional district. Circulators there can only petition in the county they live in and an adjacent county.
- In Illinois, a new party needs 25,000 signatures to get on the ballot, while "established parties" only need 5,000 signatures.
- In Oklahoma, 36,202 signatures are required for a candidate to qualify for the ballot. With a population of 3,350,000, Oklahoma ranks 28th in the nation in population, but its total signature requirement is the fourth highest in the United States and the highest per capita in the country.
- Oklahoma (along with South Dakota) doesn't allow write-in votes, which strikes us as a lawsuit waiting to happen.

Those are just the raw number barriers. But there are also excessive filing fees, early deadlines, and administrative hurdles. For example, in Pennsylvania, the state requires signature forms on special colored paper; it only provided four hundred forms though our volunteers needed more than two thousand. The state would not accept forms downloaded from the Internet. In West Virginia and Georgia, the filing fee is $4,000! In Michigan, petition forms had to be on odd-sized paper (8-1/2 by 13 inches).

In many states, our petitioners were harassed and threatened with arrest by officials with a shallow understanding of the First Amendment for circulating petitions in public places or taxpayer-financed parks and recreation areas. In Mississippi, the mayor of Tupelo stopped our petitioners from working in the town square at a festival on the Fourth of July. In Ohio, our petitioners were stopped from collecting signatures at a public market in West Cleveland. The reports from our volunteer petitioners were profiles in courage.

Of course, the Green Party is not the only one to face this challenge. The Libertarian Party, the Reform Party, the Natural Law Party, and the Constitutional Party . . . all of the third parties have to go through this charade every time they seek to compete with the established duopolists. What happens when progress is made? The Democrats and Republicans who control the state assemblies and legislatures just run back into session to make the hurdles tougher.

For these reasons, we need to encourage adoption of a model ballot law and remove barriers to entry. The Appleseed Center for Electoral Reform and the Harvard Legislative Research Bureau set forth a Model Act for the Democratization of Ballot Access[1] that includes these reforms:

- Lower signature thresholds to a reasonable level
- Eliminate outrageous filing fees
- End constraints on the identity of petitioners and signers
- Establish a filing deadline of, and allow corrections until, September 1 of election year
- Use random sampling for verification
- Eliminate so-called sore-loser bans
- Accept all write-in candidates
- Apply all reforms to independent candidates
- Allow performance in the last two elections as qualification
- Optimally, use a threshold of 0.05 percent party registration to determine ballot access.

We also suggest these additional voting reforms to engage more voters in the process:

- Adopt same-day voter registration. Just when most people get excited about politics, in the last few weeks before the election, it is too late to register to vote in most states. State and local officials should act to follow the lead of those six states that allow eligible voters to register right up to the election.
- Open up the two-party system by adopting proportional representation. Around the world, multiparty systems of proportional representation allow citizens more-direct representation in their government. Municipalities across the nation—including New York City—used proportional representation systems for years before the major parties crushed the system. There are countless opportunities at the state and local levels to reestablish this markedly more democratic system.
- Gauge public opinion at the polls by initiating a national nonbinding advisory referendum. We should put forth nonbinding referenda on salient local, state, and national issues for voting on Election Day. This would allow the public an additional mechanism to directly instruct their representatives—instead of forcing elected officials to rely on questionable commercial polls.
- Make every vote count by allowing instant runoff voting. At every government level, we should follow the lead of London and the countries of Ireland and Australia and establish a system of instant runoff voting. By allowing voters to rank candidates (see the articles in this issue of the *National Civic Review* by Castillo and McGrath, and Richie and Hill, for explanations of how this works), we can liberate citizens to choose their favorite candidate, and ignore the cries of "wasted vote" and "spoiler."

- Adopt a binding, none-of-the-above option. Voters should be able to reject unsatisfactory candidates by choosing none of the above and, if NOTA wins, force a new election with new candidates.
- Demand strict enforcement of the Voting Rights Act. The debacle in Florida highlighted the extreme need for reassessing the impact of race and class on electoral mechanics. The VRA must be enforced strictly to safeguard the basic rights of citizens across the nation.
- Accept a standardized national ballot. There would have been no butterfly-ballot controversy if state and local officials had cooperated in creating an effective standardized system for national elections.
- Make election officials nonpartisan (not bipartisan) at the local, state, and national levels. Officials usually respect the notion that democracy trumps party loyalty, but inherent in a party system is the danger that a few partisan officials will tilt the process in practice. State and local officials must establish systems by which nonpartisan officials control the all-important mechanics of election.
- Count write-in ballots in all states.
- Provide public disclosure of vote totals by precinct on the Internet.
- Provide access to voter registration forms on the Internet.
- Provide voter pamphlets online, at polling places, and by mail to voters.
- Provide nonpolitical assignment of ballot lines.

Presidential Debates

If a third-party candidate braves the Sisyphean daily task of getting a message out to the voters when almost no one in the corporate-conglomerated fourth estate is willing to provide coverage, and if the candidate spends tens of thousands of hours and dollars (in some cases millions) to overcome the ballot access hurdles, there still remains the biggest barrier of all, the traditional mechanism of reaching tens of millions of people in the age of television: participation in presidential debates. The term *presidential debate* is almost a quaint misnomer considering the love fest of agreement and the exercise in diversion displayed between the major-party candidates during those encounters held last fall. The gatekeeper for the viewing voters is a little-known entity called the Commission on Presidential Debates (CPD).

The Commission on Presidential Debates

In 1907, Congress enacted the Tillman Act, prohibiting corporate contributions to any candidate running for federal office. In the early 1970s, Congress enacted the Federal Election Campaign Act (FECA), which, in part, created an administrative agency, the Federal Election Commission (FEC), to enforce the act's campaign finance and disclosure laws, which include the 1907 prohibition on corporate contributions to federal campaigns. Under these laws, for-profit corporations are *not* allowed to spend money "in connection with" campaigns for federal office, unless the money is used for "nonpartisan activity."

Pursuant to the FECA, which should really be renamed the Duopoly Protection Act, the FEC in the late 1970s told the League of Women Voters (who used to sponsor the presidential debates) that they could not accept money from corporations to help defray the cost of debates.

In 1987, the Democratic and Republican Parties decided to take over the sponsorship of the debates by creating their own commission. Notably, the CPD is run by the former chairmen of the Democratic and Republican parties. After the CPD was established, the FEC (whose commission is composed of three Democrats and three Republicans) rejected its own general counsel's opinion, reversed its prior position, and adopted a regulation that allows corporations to spend money to help stage federal candidate debates.

This loophole created in the regulatory framework established by Congress allows corporate money to tilt the electoral playing field for the two major party candidates. It is our position that the FEC regulation exceeds the statutory authority granted by Congress and should be struck down. The National Voting Rights Institute and pro bono lawyers are currently asking the U.S. Supreme Court to consider the legality of this regulation.

If this legal challenge is successful, corporate sponsors of the CPD debates—which include beer and tobacco companies—would again be subject to the FECA's corporate contribution prohibition. We would then have presidential debates that do not look like Bud bowls filled with corporate logos and an Anheuser-Busch beer tent. In the age of the Invesco Stadium, the Fleet Center, the Target Center, the United Center, and other exercises in corporate naming, can we still imagine any sort of competition not replete with corporate advertisements even when the point is to elect the president of the United States?

Adding insult to injury, eligibility for getting a message out entails permission from a bipartisan commission, funded by beer and tobacco money, that sets an arbitrary standard of reaching a 15 percent rating in five polls of the commission's choosing—polls whose major media parent companies have executives who give lots of money to the duopolists. With these criteria, Abraham Lincoln would have been excluded from the debates; he wasn't even on the ballot in nine states. The debate commission made a mistake, from their viewpoint, by letting Ross Perot into the debates in 1992. The viewership shot up to more than ninety million Americans, and Perot got 19 percent of the vote. But four years later, after the Clinton and Dole camps decided to exclude Perot, network viewership plummeted to forty-two million.

Another independent candidate, Jesse Ventura, got into the gubernatorial debates in Minnesota in 1998, and he became the governor. It was clear during the 2000 presidential election that the Republicans and the Democrats were not prepared to make this mistake again. We received a polite letter saying we didn't meet their self-serving criteria for participation. Who knew that the gatekeepers to the American presidency's electorate sit in a private office in Washington, D.C.?

Indeed, the commission was so terrified of competition they would not even let Ralph Nader physically near the debates. In October 2000, for the first debate at the University of Massachusetts, he had a ticket to get into the auditorium adjacent to the scene of the debates, but the CPD decided to use state troopers to keep him from listening to the debates and from talking to the media at the media trailer—despite the fact that the media had invited him to do so. There are countries abroad that we criticize for this kind of authoritarian behavior. We filed a lawsuit in connection with this action; earlier this year, the federal judge in Boston hearing the case denied the CPD's motion to dismiss.

No coverage, awful ballot laws, no access to the voters through debates . . . in the economic world, we would call each of these a barrier to entry that distorts the market from perfect competition. Imagine if we told entrepreneurs that before they were allowed to compete they had to have a 15 percent market share. You can be sure that there would be antitrust suits.

Between the ballot access hurdles and the debate commission, Nader 2000 brought eleven lawsuits in a nine-month campaign thanks to the help of the Brennan Center for Justice at NYU Law School, the National Voting Rights Institute, and pro bono law firms. We had to arrange for the equivalent of a full-time public-interest law firm just to level the playing ground to compete.

This does not even count the need to defend. In a striking case of corporate immolation worthy of a case study at the Harvard Business School, MasterCard decided to sue us for daring to parody their "Priceless" ad campaign in noncommercial use of our campaign finance spoof on the "things money can't buy"—a spot that was designed to move poll numbers and get Nader into the debates. Apparently, MasterCard doesn't share our sense of humor, and although they lost their attempt at a temporary restraining order, they are continuing to sue us even after the election for alleged copyright and trademark infringement.

Campaigns, of course, are not priceless. More than half a billion dollars was raised in soft money by the parties in the last election cycle. *The Washington Post* in February 2001 editorialized that "the campaign finance system is totally out of control. . . . In each of the last two presidential cycles, the amount [of soft money] has doubled. . . . If officeholders aren't being bought by such sums, the offices themselves surely are."[2]

The biggest obstacle to just government action is the corruption of our election campaigns by special-interest money. No one should have to sell out to big business or big donors to run a competitive campaign. Political campaigns should be publicly financed, just like public libraries, parks, and schools. We started the campaign with a $40,000 personal contribution by the candidate. Our average donation was less than $100. We raised a little over $8 million in nine months, taking no corporate money, no PAC money, and no soft money, and we did our frugal best to run a nationwide campaign with the energy of volunteers and the Green Party. To put it into perspective, the Democratic Party spent $8 million advertising in the state of Michigan alone.

To remove barriers to entry for third parties, we need to end legalized bribery and support publicly financed campaigns. The McCain-Feingold Bill that is pending as this article was being written is not the solution to dirty-money politics. Although it eliminates soft money, the bill raises hard-money limits, does not provide free airtime for candidates, and does not establish public financing. Therefore, the barriers to entry for serious candidates will remain.

If a candidate overcomes all of these structural barriers, there still remain a host of other problems, such as the bias in favor of the two-party system that we are taught in school, straw polls that do not include any of the other parties (Libertarian Party, Reform Party, Constitution Party, Green Party), and the influence of parental voting patterns. Hereditary voting practices have made voting for a third party an extraordinary political act. Third parties are viewed as freak institutions because the United States doesn't have proportional representation or instant runoff voting as other countries do, and because people are generally unaware of how third parties have advanced justice in this country by raising such radical ideas as abolition of slavery, women's suffrage, the graduated income tax, and deficit reduction.

In the mid-nineteenth century, it took just six years for the Republicans to replace the Whigs as an emerging major party. Given the structural hurdles in place favoring the Democratic and Republican parties, what would it take for a startup to replace either of these entrenched parties today?

What is the price we pay for our forgone democracy? What does it cost us in efforts not undertaken and social justice left unrealized? Currently in the United States, there are thirty-eight million poor people, 20 percent of children live in deep poverty, 80 percent of workers have lost ground since 1973 (after adjusting wages for inflation), forty-six million people are without health insurance, there is a record level of personal bankruptcy, and total consumer debt is more than $6 trillion.

Our country faces critical housing needs, crumbling public works, global warming, forest destruction, air and water pollution, rampant corporate fraud, and numerous public health problems, all against a backdrop of sprawl and gated communities, billions spent on campaigns, a burgeoning prison industry with more than two million people incarcerated, a failed war on drugs, more than one hundred million eligible voters who do not vote, and states that cannot even process the votes of those who do.

Our two-party political system is engaged in an unfair restraint of democratic participation. It is a duopoly that has erected barriers to political engagement and is restricting the exercise of democracy in our country. Our laws do not countenance such an illegitimate concentration of power in the economy. Do we hold our political and democratic values in lesser esteem?

Notes

1. In the *Harvard Journal on Legislation,* Summer 1999, 36 (2), 451–478.
2. *Washington Post* editorial, Feb. 19, 2001, p. A32.

Ralph Nader was the Green Party candidate for president in the 2000 election.

Theresa Amato was the campaign manager of the national Nader 2000 campaign.

Who Should Elect the President?
The Case Against the Electoral
College

Carolyn Jefferson-Jenkins

We the people do not directly elect the president of the United States; the electoral college does. This election method may satisfy some people, but a desire for change is in the air. In Congress, in state legislatures, in newspapers, in magazines, and on television, the issue of electoral college reform is being widely discussed.

The crux of the problem—for which every thinking citizen should have an informed answer—is this: What method of electing the president best serves the people of the United States in the twenty-first century? The electoral college, a curious vestige of the eighteenth century, violates the principle of one person, one vote. The time has come to abolish it.

When the founders set up that system, democracy was practiced differently from today. Women could not vote; African Americans could not vote; people without property could not vote. The men who wrote the Constitution were deeply mistrustful of popular opinion. Hence they set up the electoral college, theoretically composed of wise and prudent men who could be trusted with the job of picking a president. U.S. senators weren't chosen directly by the people, either; state legislatures did that.

But in the two centuries since, the franchise has greatly expanded. Blacks won the constitutional right to vote in 1870, women in 1920, and eighteen-year-olds in 1971. Senate races yielded to direct election early in the twentieth century. Today, with universal public education, newspapers, radio, television, and the Internet, citizens can see and hear candidates in a way unimaginable in 1787. The idea that the people aren't qualified to choose their president directly does not hold up. The course of American history has been inexorably toward greater fairness, uniformity, and inclusiveness in our democracy. Yet the system for electing the most important representative of the American people is stuck in a time warp.

Among the arguments advanced in favor of keeping the electoral college are that it protects the interests of the states, especially small states; that it's a key part of our federal system; and that minorities and others in large urban areas would lose influence without it. The argument for abolishing it, in favor of direct election of the president, is that the electoral college violates the fundamental principle of one person, one vote. I explore these arguments in detail in this article. But the important fact to stress at the outset is that simple fairness demands change. We need to trust the voters in a way that the founders, two centuries ago, did not.

The Electoral College Method

Before judgment can be made as to whether or not the electoral college method of electing the president should be changed, its merits and deficiencies must be identified and evaluated. For a thorough assessment, it is necessary to know something about the circumstances under which the system was established, what sort of change has occurred since its inception, and how the system operates now.

Article II, Section 1, of the Constitution states that the president shall be chosen by a group of electors appointed in each state, in a manner prescribed by the state legislatures, equal to the number of senators and representatives of each state in Congress. It assigns the counting of electoral votes to Congress and provides for the election of a president by the House of Representatives and of a vice president by the Senate in case either one does not receive the votes of a majority of the electoral college. Currently, the magic number for a majority of electors is 270.

The idea of a strong, elected executive for a nation was completely revolutionary in 1787, when the Constitution was written. The United States of America was held together by loose Articles of Confederation that included no provision for any executive department. Crown-appointed colonial governors had been succeeded by weak executives chosen by strong state legislatures. Fear of monarchy was still very much alive.

Only indirectly do we the people choose the president of the United States every four years. The choosing process has developed into a mixture of procedures born of a complicated ancestry: the Constitution, state laws, political parties, rules and customs, political expediency, and mere tradition.

The first three and most visible steps in the process are (1) campaigns by presidential candidates in state primaries and caucuses for delegates to the national party conventions, (2) selection of nominees for president by national conventions in the summer of a presidential election year, and (3) conduct of campaigns by nominees for the people's votes in the general election. But well before Election Day in November, the less visible parts of the process get under way.

First, political parties in each state nominate, by convention, committee, primary, or in some instances petition, groups of presidential electors, equal to the number of senators and representatives each state has in Congress (the District of Columbia gets three). Presidential electors as a group have come to be known as the electoral college, even though it never meets as a national body.

Then, on Election Day—the first Tuesday after the first Monday in November of a presidential election year—the people in each state select, by a simple plurality, the group of presidential electors pledged to one of the candidates. The people do not vote to choose a president but rather to choose electors who will choose one.

In the period between election of the electors and their casting of electoral votes, bargaining for electoral votes can take place because under the Constitution the electors are free agents. Within each state, the winning group of presidential electors meets in the state capital on the first Monday following the second Wednesday in December. Each elector normally casts one vote for the presidential nominee of his or her party. Almost always, electors vote automatically rather than independently—in some states by custom and in others by party pledge or state law.

In every state except two (Maine and Nebraska, which allot their electors proportionally by congressional district), all of a state's electoral votes are cast for the winner of the popular vote. Ballots cast for the losing candidate aren't counted at all in the electoral sweepstakes. This winner-take-all system serves to disenfranchise those who voted for the candidate who lost their state.

Results of the mid-December voting in each state are sent to the Congress. On January 6, in the presence of the Senate and the House, the electoral vote total for each presidential nominee is enumerated and officially announced. If one nominee receives the votes of a majority of the presidential electors—270 votes out of 538—a president has been elected. If no nominee receives the votes of a majority of the electors, the House of Representatives chooses the president from among the three top presidential vote getters in the electoral college.

To win, a nominee must get a majority of the votes cast. Each state delegation in the House has only one vote; but if the delegation is evenly divided, it loses the vote. Since a quorum for this election is "a member or member from two-thirds of the states," it is possible that thirty-four members of the House of Representatives could constitute the body to decide on a president.

First submitted in Congress in 1797, reform of the electoral college system is the most frequently proposed constitutional reform. More than a thousand bills—many of them constitutional amendments—have been introduced in Congress to change how we elect our presidents. Why has success for any kind of reform been so elusive?

It is difficult to amend the U.S. Constitution. In the case of reforming the electoral college system it has been impossible for members of the jurisdictional committees of Congress, let alone all of Congress, to agree on a method. The right combination of pressure, people, politics, and priorities that must exist to get a constitutional amendment through Congress has not yet occurred.

Major Policy Questions: Choices to Be Made

Electoral college reform is a complex, multifaceted subject, involving judgment concerning political principles as well as decisions about practical measures and the likely effect of any proposed revision. Using the electoral college to elect the president is a state-related intermediate step between the act of voting by the people and actual election of the president. A preliminary question for consideration is whether, in the matter of electing the president, one is willing to accept any alteration in the relationships among the people of the United States, the states, and the national government from how the Constitution designated these relationships in 1787.

If one is dissatisfied with the status quo but unwilling to consider any alteration in these relationships, then one must consider reform in terms of modification within the existing system. For those who desire substantial change, the principal choice is whether or not there should be a state-related step. In other words, should the electoral vote be retained, or should some other technique be designed to involve voters directly? If one chooses to retain the electoral vote, then one must make other choices about its allocation and counting and whether there should be electors to cast the electoral votes. The basic alternative to a process with a state-related step is direct popular vote. This alternative means that states, as units, would have no direct role in a presidential election. They would have only an indirect role, that of setting voting qualifications and administering the election itself.

This discussion of electoral college reform considers three major policy questions. First, how should federalism, states' rights, and the popular will relate to electing the president? Second, what should the roles of the federal government and the states be regarding voting qualifications and actual conduct of a presidential election? Third, what effect on political parties does direct popular election of the president have?

Federalism, States' Rights, and the Popular Will. Awareness of how indirectly the people of this country elect their president comes as a shock to most people. Less well known is the fact that a popular vote for the president, direct or indirect, is not embedded in the Constitution and therefore theoretically could disappear in any state, or all states, at any time. Just last December, the Florida legislature was prepared to nullify the popular vote, the outcome of which was still in contention, and name its own slate of electors—although it stopped short of taking that step. That the states now "appoint" their presidential electors by a statewide popular vote is political happenstance.

In the minds of some, there is a question of whether our form of government as a federal republic is safeguarded by having the electoral college. According to this view, the fact that this country is a federation of states, and that the Constitution assigns certain powers to the federal government while others remain with the states, is of more importance than direct election of the president based on the principle of one person, one vote. Others believe that a decisive role for the states was appropriate for a fledgling federal government in 1787, but perhaps a different balance is needed in the twenty-first century to preserve the freedoms outlined two hundred years earlier.

Another question pertaining to federalism is whether there is still a basic conflict in this country between the interests of large and small states. Some people believe that although there were substantial differences when the Constitution was written, in this century the interests of the people of a small state as far as electing a president are concerned parallel those of the people of a more populous state. Others believe that a basic conflict still exists—and they use that conviction in arguing for keeping a state-related step in electing a president.

The One-Person, One-Vote Principle. The one-person, one-vote concept of political equality set out in the U.S. Supreme Court case *Gray v. Sanders* is often cited by those who believe that an intermediate state-related step—with or without a winner-take-all method of allocating electoral votes—creates inequality among voters in a presidential election.

One person, one vote is the guiding principle of our representative democracy. Through decades of struggle, this principle has now been established for elective offices across the land. The Constitution originally provided for the Senate to be elected by state legislatures. The Seventeenth Amendment, ratified in 1913, codified direct election by the people of the states. *Reynolds v. Sims* (1964) required that state legislatures follow the principle of one person, one vote. Other cases required application of this principle to other elected offices, including the House of Representatives.

The Winner-Take-All System. The winner-take-all system, in which all of a state's electoral votes go to the winner of the popular vote, disenfranchises those who voted for other candidates in that state. Their votes simply don't count. This fact lessens voter turnout and affects how campaigns are run. If one or the other major party is traditionally victorious in a particular state, there is arguably less motivation for a citizen in that state to vote, no matter which candidate he or she might support. If that party customarily wins, why bother to vote? If it customarily loses, again, why vote? Supporters of third-party candidates face even more daunting prospects. The campaign focus on swing states with a large number of electoral votes may also exert a depressive effect on voter turnout as many other states receive only minimal attention at best from the major-party candidates.

Lose the Popular Vote, Win the Presidency. Finally, the fact that votes for the losing candidates in each state don't count, can—and as recently as Election 2000 has—resulted in the victory of a president who lost the nationwide popular vote.

This can happen only if there is a state-related step in the election process. Therefore, the only reform proposal that prevents this outcome is direct election of the president. Whether the possibility of a nonplurality president should be a great concern is frequently debated. Some people feel the country does not unite behind such a president and the national stability is therefore endangered. Others are convinced that a slight margin of the popular vote one way or another won't harm the nation's political health.

The Federal Role in National Elections

The choices to be made in regard to the federal role in a national election concern setting voter qualifications for the presidential election and the conduct of the election, especially counting the votes and setting standards for a vote challenge. These considerations come to the fore when a direct popular election is under discussion.

Conduct of the Election and Counting of Votes. Since the federal government has no existing election machinery, it is likely that states would continue to conduct presidential elections if the country decided on a system of direct popular election. As far as counting the votes is concerned, U.S. Supreme Court decisions and civil rights legislation have established the federal right to intervene in the states' conduct of a federal election in matters relating to fraud. But recourse through the courts does not satisfy some advocates of the direct popular vote, who desire a uniform and nationally policed system for a presidential election. Opponents of such a system, such as the American Jewish Congress, contend that oversight of the voting process by the federal government is inconsistent with federalism. Others believe that a constitutional amendment setting up a uniform and nationally policed system for presidential elections would be a natural next step in developing the principle of one person, one vote. Still others don't agree that the federal government has to assume a comprehensive role in conducting a presidential election.

Opponents of the direct popular vote for president stress the possibility of endless delays caused by multiple recounts. Advocates of the popular vote, on the other hand, declare that there can be equal uncertainty under the current system if recounts are needed in large, pivotal states, such as Florida in 2000. Some people believe the federal government should set standards for acceptable reasons for contesting a vote and for resolving challenges, including a specific time limit for resolution.

Voter Qualifications. The principal controversy regarding voter qualification raised by the prospect of direct popular election of the president concerns who should set the standards, the federal government or the states.

In Article I, Section 4 of the Constitution, responsibility for prescribing the time, place, and manner of holding an election for senators and representatives is given to the legislature of each state, "but the Congress may at any time by law make or alter such regulations, except as to the places of choosing senators."

Since the Constitution also gives legislatures the power to decide how presidential electors are chosen, to date they have set the qualifications for voting in a presidential election. A number of resolutions have been introduced in Congress, however, to amend the Constitution by setting federal qualifications of various kinds, such as age and residency.

Effects on Political Parties of Direct Popular Election of the President

Partly because political parties were not yet in existence when the Constitution was written, their development has had a profound effect on the presidential election process. Methods of nominating presidential candidates and campaigning for election owe their present form to the ways in which political parties have evolved. Conversely, the electoral college system has had a profound effect on the two-party system. Any change in the method of election would leave a deep mark on our major political parties, on splinter parties and their possible proliferation, on how candidates are nominated, and on how they campaign. Most political observers want to see the two-party system preserved no matter what reforms are adopted. Proponents of the direct popular vote say this system would not encourage proliferation of splinter parties.

Direct Election Is the Most Representative System

In the summer of 1968, the League of Women Voters began a study of the electoral college to determine whether changes needed to be made in the method of electing the president. The results of this study are the foundation for our position that direct popular election of the president is the best method for a system of representative government that is responsive to the will of the people. Leagues in more than one thousand communities across the country participated in the study and came to the same conclusion.

Since 1970, the league has supported amending the Constitution to abolish the electoral college and establish direct popular vote for the president and vice president of the United States. Political developments since the 1970s have only underscored the need to eliminate the electoral college system. The downward trend in voter participation, coupled with increased cynicism and skepticism among the public as to the ability of elected leaders to provide meaningful representation, were all warning signs prior to the startling developments of Election 2000.

We no longer need to imagine what it would be like to have one candidate win the popular vote and another candidate win the presidency. Such an outcome has happened in the past, in 1824, 1876, and 1888. In Election 2000, history repeated itself. Like Rutherford B. Hayes more than a century earlier, George W. Bush lost the popular vote but won the White House. We all saw the public confusion—and the outrage among voters who felt that Al Gore, who won the popular tally by more than five hundred thousand votes, shouldn't have ended up as the loser.

Now let's go one step further. Consider a close race for president in which no candidate earns the necessary electoral college votes to win. This has happened twice before in our nation's history, in the elections of 1800 and 1824, when the House of Representatives chose Thomas Jefferson and John Quincy Adams, respectively. The league believes both of these men were fine presidents, but we are deeply troubled by the prospect that some future winner of the popular vote could lose the election in a House dominated by one or another political party.

In the twentieth century, we only narrowly avoided a series of constitutional crises in which the electoral college system—or the House of Representatives—could have overruled the popular vote:

- In the 1916 presidential election, a shift of only 2,000 votes in California would have given Charles Evans Hughes the necessary electoral votes to defeat Woodrow Wilson, despite Wilson's half-million-vote plurality nation-wide.
- In 1948, a shift of only 30,000 votes in three states would have delivered the White House to Governor Dewey, in spite of the fact that he trailed President Truman by some 2.1 million popular votes.
- In 1960, a shift of only 13,000 votes in five states would have made Richard Nixon president.
- In 1968, a shift of 42,000 votes in three states (Alaska, Missouri, and New Jersey) would have denied Nixon an electoral college victory and thrown the election into the House of Representatives.
- In 1976, a shift of only 9,300 votes would have elected Gerald Ford, even though he trailed Jimmy Carter in the popular vote by 1.6 million ballots.

Three Reasons the Current System Is Unfair

In testimony before Congress in 1997, the League of Women Voters pointed out that apart from the public outcry that would be caused by circumvention of the popular will, there are a number of other serious flaws in the electoral college system. The electoral college system is fundamentally unfair to voters. In a nation where voting rights are grounded in the one-person, one-vote principle, the electoral college is a hopeless anachronism.

First, a citizen's individual vote has more weight if he or she lives in a state with a small population than if the citizen lives in a state with a large population. Moreover, the electoral vote does not reflect the volume of voter participation within a state. If only a few voters go to the polls, all the electoral votes of the state are still cast. Finally, the electoral college system is flawed because the Constitution does not bind presidential electors to vote for the candidates to whom they have been pledged. For example, in 1972, 1976, 1988, and 2000, individual electors who were pledged to one of the top two vote-getters cast blank ballots or voted for also-rans. "Faithless electors" in a close race could cause a crisis of confidence in our electoral system.

For all these reasons, the league believes that the presidential election method should incorporate the one-person, one-vote principle. The president should be directly elected by the people he or she will represent, just as other federally elected officials are in this country. Direct election is the most representative system. It is the only system that guarantees the president will have received the most popular votes. It also encourages voter participation by giving voters a direct and equal role in electing the president. Of course, a direct popular vote does not preclude the possibility of a close three-way race in which no candidate receives a majority of the votes. The league believes that if no candidate receives more than 40 percent of the popular vote, then a national runoff election should be held.

Any substantial change in the method of electing the president and vice president must be accomplished through amending the U.S. Constitution, which requires a two-thirds vote of both the U.S. Senate and the U.S. House of Representatives followed by ratification by the legislatures of three-fourths of the states. But what if amending the Constitution proves politically impossible? Reforming the electoral college can be done without changing the Constitution. Until there is a constitutional amendment to abolish the electoral college, the league supports prompt establishment of clear rules and procedures for the House and Senate to handle their responsibilities in electing the president and vice president if no one receives a majority in the electoral college.

Other proposals short of a constitutional amendment could make it more likely that the electoral vote reflects the popular vote. States could act, on their own, to make a variety of changes. Some reformers warn, however, that state-by-state actions might give us a crazy quilt of election laws that make things even more complicated. They argue that either all the states should do the same thing, or things are better left as they are.

States could, if they wanted, make these changes:

- *Congressional district proportionality.* Each congressional district elects one elector. The two "Senate" electors are apportioned to the statewide winner. (There's a downside to this method, however. Redrawing Congressional districts—old-fashioned gerrymandering—is raised to the presidential level. With the Senate electors going to the statewide winner, it is still a winner-take-most system.)
- *Statewide proportionality.* The number of electors within a state is awarded in proportion to each candidate's statewide totals.
- *Binding of electors.* Electors might be required by law (with penalties attached for noncompliance) to vote for their candidate, ending the unpredictable effect of the faithless elector.
- *Abolition of electors.* Abolition requires a constitutional amendment. We recognize that it is extraordinarily difficult to amend the Constitution; the league had seventy-two years of experience in trying to win the right for women to vote. Nevertheless, the time for change has come. We urge the House and Senate to pass a constitutional amendment abolishing the electoral college and letting Americans, for the first time ever, vote directly for their president.

Carolyn Jefferson-Jenkins is the president of the League of Women Voters of the United States.

Renewed Momentum for Voting System Reform

Rob Richie, Steven Hill

For decades the National Civic League, and its predecessor the National Municipal League, has touted reform of the plurality-wins-all voting rules typical of U.S. elections. After remarkable successes—including implementation of the choice voting form of proportional representation (PR) in such major cities as Cleveland, Cincinnati, New York, and Sacramento—the voting system reform movement ultimately waned because of a combination of hostility from old-style political machines, election administration barriers, and Cold War–driven suspicion of representation of political and racial minorities.

Today, instant runoff voting (IRV) and PR have reemerged as two critical reforms for those interested in fair representation and better elections. The renewed interest in these reforms suggests their appeal and underscores the flexibility reformers must often have if they are to succeed.

IRV simulates a series of runoff elections, but in a single round of voting; thus it is faster, cheaper, and better (in terms of turnout) than two-round runoffs. At the polls, people vote for their favorite candidate but can also rank all the candidates in order of preference. If a candidate receives a majority of first-choice votes, the election is over. If no candidate wins a majority on the first round of counting, the candidate with the fewest votes is eliminated, and a second round of counting occurs. In this round, the second-choice preferences on ballots for the now-eliminated candidate are counted as first-choice votes. The counting continues until a majority winner is determined. The electoral majority is no longer fractured by a spoiler candidacy.

In 1996, when the Center for Voting and Democracy coined the name of the system, there essentially was no awareness of, let alone support, for the idea of instant runoff voting among Americans. No state or federal legislation had been introduced on IRV in decades, no city had voted on implementing it since 1974, and it was rarely discussed in civic circles. Since then, despite relatively small resources backing activity on its behalf, support has grown exponentially. This article discusses some examples.

In November 2000, Oakland, California, adopted a city charter amendment to use IRV in special elections to fill a vacancy on the city council. Also in that month, voters in San Leandro, California, joined Santa Clara County

(California) and Vancouver, Washington, in approving legislation to allow use of IRV in local elections. Pursuant to recommendation by commissions in the respective jurisdictions, there is a strong likelihood that measures will be on the ballot in 2001 to implement IRV for city elections in Austin, Texas; Berkeley, California; and Eugene, Oregon.

Bills supporting IRV have been introduced in a dozen state legislatures in 2001, including bipartisan bills to use IRV for statewide election in Washington State and Vermont and a bill introduced by the speaker of California's Assembly, Robert Hertzberg, to adopt IRV for vacancy election for federal and state legislative seats. A ballot measure to adopt IRV for nearly all state and federal races has qualified for the November 2002 ballot in Alaska. At the federal level, there are two bills that call for studying or supporting IRV (including one, H.R. 57, with nearly fifty cosponsors) and at least two additional pro-IRV bills are expected.

A broad range of political and opinion leaders—elected office holders, election officials, journalists, media organizations, and civic leaders—publicly support IRV. Newspaper endorsements have come from *USA Today*, the *St. Petersburg Times*, the *Trenton Times*, the *Vancouver Columbian*, the *Mercury News*, and the *Sacramento Bee*. Major articles and commentary about IRV have appeared in such publications as the *New York Times*, the *Wall Street Journal*, and the *Washington Post;* organizations endorsing IRV include the Sierra Club, U.S. Public Interest Research Group, and several state branches of Common Cause and the League of Women Voters.

In 2000, IRV was used in two presidential nominations (the Reform Party and Green Party) and in one county commission nomination (the Republican Party in Summit County, Utah); Utah Republicans will likely use IRV at their 2001 state convention.

These advances would not have happened if IRV did not make such good sense, but reformers have also had to capitalize on conditions that made elected officials open to reform. For better or worse, political reforms are opportunity-driven; that is, reform must be seen as the solution to a problem that needs to be fixed.

For instance, the major parties dislike the spoiler problem by which one of their candidates loses as a result of a third-party candidacy splitting their vote. In recent years, both Republicans and Democrats have been "spoiled" by third-party candidates in high-profile races; arguably, Ross Perot cost George Bush the 1992 presidential election and Ralph Nader cost Al Gore the 2000 election. Third parties tipped a U.S. Senate race in Washington State, the contest for the governor's seat in Alaska, and several U.S. House races.

In New Mexico, where Green Party candidates have spoiled outcomes for Democrats in the gubernatorial and several congressional races, leading Democrats support IRV. Legislation to place a sweeping pro-IRV measure on the ballot passed the state senate in 1999—less than two years after this voting-reform system received its first attention in the state—before dying in the state house.

IRV is still alive in New Mexico, but backers must focus on how to help the state get modern voting machines that can handle an IRV election.

In Alaska, the Republican Party is making IRV its number one priority because, largely thanks to split votes in both primary and general elections, the GOP has not held the governor's mansion for more than two decades. Reformers have gathered enough signatures to place a measure on the November 2002 ballot to adopt IRV for nearly all state offices.

In Vermont, the groundwork for IRV is well laid. The Democrats, who foresee being spoiled by the growing Progressive Party, are easier to convince than Republicans, who face a seemingly less significant threat from the smaller Libertarian Party. But the state also has a compelling good-government reason to enact IRV: if no candidate wins the governor's race with an outright majority, the state constitution requires that the governor be elected by the legislature. (Such an outcome occurred last year in Mississippi's gubernatorial race.) Given the state's new public financing law for the governor's race, third-party candidates have a better chance to win funding and votes, thereby increasing the chances for a plurality outcome.

The Vermont House of Representatives passed a resolution establishing a special citizens' commission to study IRV. The commission, including members of the League of Women Voters and Common Cause and covering the entire tripartisan political spectrum, issued a report that unanimously recommended IRV for all statewide elections. Governor Howard Dean has endorsed IRV; other endorsing groups range from the generally conservative Vermont Grange to the Vermont Public Interest Research Group. The bill has excellent prospects for 2002, and other states with new public-financing laws are also showing interest in IRV.

An obvious angle for IRV is that many local and primary elections—including nearly all federal primaries in the South—use two-round runoff elections that are expensive for both taxpayers and candidates who have to pay for two elections. A traditional runoff undermines the goal of campaign finance reform, and voter fatigue often leads to a drop in voter turnout. In Austin, a charter commission has recommended replacing two-round runoffs with IRV. Other jurisdictions focusing on this aspect of IRV include San Francisco, Santa Clara County, and Eugene. On the flip side, an Albuquerque, New Mexico, charter commission recommended IRV for local elections after the mayoral race was won with only 29 percent of the vote, in the absence of a runoff law.

Sometimes courts create a situation generating interest in alternate voting systems. For example, last year the U.S. Supreme Court overturned states' authority to force political parties to use a "blanket primary" in which voters can support any candidate they want, regardless of party, in each primary election. Washington and California were affected, causing a surge of interest in IRV. IRV would increase voters' options both in primaries and general elections, helping to balance any loss of choice from eliminating blanket primaries. Introduced for the first time in 2001, Washington's IRV bill lasted longer than any other bill seeking to address the blanket primary dilemma.

The courts have also created opportunities for using voting systems such as cumulative voting as an alternative to single-member districts for achieving fair racial representation. Under a cumulative voting system, there are multi-member rather than single-member districts. Each voter casts as many votes as there are members for the district. In a hypothetical instance, for a district in which six candidates are running for three seats, voters can vote for three candidates, or give all three of their votes to a single candidate, or give two votes to one candidate and the remaining vote to another candidate.

In numerous states (Texas, North Carolina, Illinois, and Alabama), consent decrees in cases brought under the Voting Rights Act have resulted in proportional systems. This has typically occurred in areas where racial minority voters were too geographically dispersed to benefit from creating a minority opportunity district. New York City uses the fully proportional system known as choice voting for school board elections; they are often the only elections in the city where geographically dispersed Asian Americans win representation. Recently, Amarillo became the largest city in Texas to use cumulative voting. In the first school board election held under this system, in May 2000, an African American was elected for the first time, and the first Latino won since the 1970s. Texas now has more than fifty localities that use an alternative voting system as a result of court action in voting rights cases.

Although not linked to voting rights issues, the Drive to Revive campaign in Illinois is an effort to restore cumulative voting at the state level. For 110 years, until 1980, the state used cumulative voting in three-seat districts to elect its state house. Interviews with current and former Illinois political leaders who were first elected under the cumulative voting system reveal several potential benefits: less regional polarization between cities and suburbs, less partisan rancor, and a broader political spectrum. Candidates of all stripes, ranging from progressive Democrats to Chicago Republicans (and independent-minded legislators, including Congressmen Paul Simon, Abner Mikva, Henry Hyde, and John Porter), got their start in the state house under this system. The *Chicago Tribune,* current and former governors, and several party leaders in the legislature have endorsed the Drive to Revive campaign.

Finally, even the recent U.S. Supreme Court rulings overturning districts drawn for racial representation, although unfortunate and misguided, have created opportunity for proposing proportional voting methods as a means to fulfill the goals of the Voting Rights Act. Using larger congressional districts with three to five representatives elected by a proportional system would likely increase the number of African Americans in the House representing Virginia, North Carolina, South Carolina, Alabama, Mississippi, and Louisiana, as well as avoid the kind of costly and divisive legal challenge that has kept some states' plans in court for an entire decade.

In the short run, cities are likely to offer the greatest opportunity for voting system reform. The increasing diversity of urban areas can make it difficult for a single representative to adequately represent the various constituencies residing in his or her district or ward. Charter commissions are responsible for asking the big questions about change to their system; it is no surprise that several charter commissions—notably in Kalamazoo, Pasadena, San Francisco, and Santa Monica—have recommended reforming their voting systems in recent years.

Whatever the impetus for reform, building a movement to pass IRV or PR requires that reformers take a united-front approach. Groups such as the League of Women Voters, Common Cause, U.S. PIRG, the National Organization for Women, the Sierra Club, voting rights organizations, community organizations, third parties, and even chambers of commerce (some of which already have endorsed or are close to endorsing IRV or PR) can be brought into the effort to demand a better democracy. Reformers need to educate their own organizations and their networks about IRV and PR and then join in coalition with other community groups to pass them. Any citizen or organization believing in fair representation and majority rule can become an advocate.

Rob Richie is the executive director of the Center for Voting and Democracy.

Steven Hill is the western regional director of the Center for Voting and Democracy.

Voting Reforms After Florida

Caleb Kleppner

Whatever else might be said about last November's election in Florida, it was certainly an educational experience. The country and the world were introduced to the lexicon of American election administration—punch cards, butterfly ballots, hanging chads—and to surprising aspects of the U.S. Constitution and American jurisprudence.

Americans who had not paid attention in social studies class learned that something called the electoral college, and not the voters, actually chooses the president of the United States. A candidate can win the popular vote but lose the election. Americans who listened closely to Supreme Court pronouncements learned that they did not have a right to vote for president. The Cwonstitution delegates this power to the state legislatures, who in turn determine the manner of choosing members of the electoral college.

But perhaps more important than these lessons was the most obvious one: all aspects of election administration have enormous room for improvement. Fortunately, the Florida debacle, along with lesser-publicized snafus in Missouri, New Mexico, Illinois, Pennsylvania, and elsewhere, sparked a healthy and overdue examination of election practices around the country.

A national consensus to improve elections has emerged. The National Council of State Legislatures (NCSL) reports that more than fifteen hundred election reform bills have already been introduced in state legislatures. (The NCSL has catalogued these bills in an online database with some sixty subtopics, at www.ncsl.org.) Congress is considering numerous bills, including a host of constitutional amendments, and municipalities are debating countless proposals for electoral reform. This newfound commitment to the electoral process is surely healthy for our democracy. In this article, I summarize the principal flaws of the recent election and then discuss what is being done at the local, state, and federal levels to correct them.

What Went Wrong

The voting process in Florida will long be remembered for its catalogue of errors. At this remove they can be briefly recounted, but it is nonetheless remarkable how extensive the list is. The most publicized problems were confusing ballot design, voting equipment that didn't count accurately, and punch cards that weren't cleanly punched. Beyond these more or less technical problems, there were an array of human failures ranging from improper or imprecise standards for purging ex-felons and others from the voting rolls to questionable practices by poll workers, possible intimidation by police officers, and general failure by state election officials to make adequate preparations to conduct the voting process. By calling the Florida outcome before polls had closed in the western part of the state, the media unhelpfully injected themselves into the proceedings. Finally, the lack of uniform standards for recounting ballots was at the core of the U.S. Supreme Court decision that eventually decided the election.

Litigation, Legislation, and Study

The country has responded to the electoral crisis in a number of ways. In several states, groups have filed lawsuits to ensure application of uniform standards, if not uniform voting equipment, in state elections. Legislation at the federal, state, and local levels is being debated now, and numerous study commissions and task forces have been formed or proposed to analyze all aspects of the election process.

Litigation. The all-important Supreme Court decision and the rest of the controversies of the election have unleashed a flood of litigation designed to ensure fair treatment of all voters. Major lawsuits addressing voting equipment and maintenance of voter registration lists have been filed in state and federal courts in Florida, Georgia, and Illinois. Many of these suits allege that disproportionate use of punch card voting equipment in communities of color violates the Constitution, the Voting Rights Act, and other state and federal laws. Especially in Florida, these suits allege wrongful purging of black voters from official voter lists and improper procedures for checking inactive voting lists. Remedies sought include decertification of punch card voting equipment, implementation of training programs designed to ensure that voting systems at polling places are fair and accurate, reform of the system used to purge ineligible voters, and appointment of federal examiners to ensure compliance.

Legislation. Elected officials are understandably reluctant about reforming the system that put them in office, especially when potholes and schools seem like more urgent budgetary priorities, but inaction in the aftermath of the last election is not a viable option. The question now is not whether reform will occur, but how much and what type.

In Congress, there is clear majority support for substantial federal funding for states and counties to upgrade voting equipment and reform election procedures. The amount and manner of providing the money to states and counties remains to be seen, but this funding will certainly prompt change in jurisdictions that otherwise could not afford it. Bills propose as much as $2.5 billion over five years, which is probably enough to put modern voting equipment in every precinct in the country that currently lacks it.

Numerous other bills have been introduced to study elections, establish federal standards for voting equipment, abolish or reform the electoral college, establish uniform poll closing times, allow proportional representation in federal elections, and more.

Modern voting equipment is generally compatible with ranked ballots and cumulative voting, which allow a jurisdiction to consider a system that represents voters more fairly than the winner-take-all system used in most American elections. The article by Richie and Hill in this issue of the *National Civic Review* discusses renewed interest in these alternate voting systems in detail. Some proposed legislation makes funding for voting equipment contingent on its compatibility with these alternatives.

In Florida, a sweeping reform bill with bipartisan support is likely to pass this year. The bill bans punch card voting equipment, requires that electronic voting equipment be programmed to reject an overvote and advise the voter of an undervote, allots $20 million in state funds to counties, requires the state to develop a standard ballot, eliminates the runoff primary in case no candidate receives a majority in the primary election, makes nonpartisan the race for supervisor of elections, authorizes a statewide database for voter registration, requires increased training and recruitment of poll workers, calls for posting a voter's bill of rights at each polling place, and ensures that voters standing in line when the polling places close are allowed to cast ballots.

Florida's legislation shows just how much can be done immediately (even before action is taken on voting equipment)—particularly in the areas of voter education and voter registration.

Study. A number of commissions and task forces have been formed or proposed in response to the election. U.S. Representatives Peter DeFazio (D-Oreg.) and Jim Leach (R-Iowa) have introduced a bill, H.R. 57, to create a Federal Elections Review Commission charged with studying all aspects of federal elections. Representative Alcee Hastings (D-Fla.) has introduced the Congress 2004 Commission Act (H.R. 506) to create a commission to study both the size of Congress and the method by which representatives are selected. In the Senate, most of the study bills also propose funding for states. These include bills by Mitch McConnell (S. 218), Tom Daschle (S. 17), Charles Schumer (S. 3273), and Arlen Specter (S. 216).

At the state level, numerous commissions have been created by both executive order and legislation. In Florida, Governor Jeb Bush convened a task force that held several public hearings and published a lengthy report of recommendations for improving Florida elections. The report and other information are available at www.collinscenter.org.

The NCSL has formed an Election Reform Task Force, which is scheduled to complete its work by August. The National Association of Counties (www.naco.org) and the National Association of State Election Directors (www.nased.org) have teamed up to create a twenty-one-member commission to review the American election process and make recommendations to improve it. The National Association of Secretaries of State (http://nass. stateofthevote.org) passed a resolution on election reform and has compiled numerous pieces of testimony by secretaries of state to their state bodies.

The nongovernment sector has been especially active. The Miller Center of Public Affairs and the Century Foundation formed the National Commission on Federal Election Reform (www.reformelections.org). Chaired by former presidents Jimmy Carter and Gerald Ford, the commission will recommend ways to improve the accuracy and fairness of federal elections. The California Institute of Technology and the Massachusetts Institute of Technology (www. vote.caltech.edu) announced a collaborative project to develop an easy-to-use, reliable, affordable, and secure voting machine to prevent recurrence of the problems that threatened the 2000 presidential election.

The Constitution Project (www.constitutionproject.org), a consensus-seeking bipartisan nonprofit organization, has launched an election reform initiative and expects to release a report this summer recommending improvements. Groups such as the National Coalition on Black Civic Participation (www. bigvote.org); the Mexican American Legal Defense and Education Fund (www.maldef.org); the National Association for the Advancement of Colored People (www.naacp.org); and many other scholars, nonprofit organizations, and concerned citizens have embarked on studies to identify problems in our electoral process and to suggest solutions.

Conclusion

Last year's election debacle crystallized public support for reform and created an unprecedented political commitment to it. Many counties and states are going to deploy modern voting equipment that makes voting easier for the voter, ensures that all votes are counted accurately, and enables jurisdictions to implement proportional representation and instant runoff voting systems. Support for reform reaches far deeper than the type of voting equipment being used. A national dialogue about all aspects of our electoral system is taking place in the media, in Congress and the state legislatures, and on countless task forces and commissions. As long as the public keeps the pressure on the elected officials, electoral reforms far beyond voting equipment will be the positive legacy of the Florida election.

Caleb Kleppner is the director of the Majority Rule Project of the Center for Voting and Democracy.

What Does It Mean to Be a Good Citizen?

Charles Bens

"We get the politicians we deserve." Can this saying be true? We might grudgingly admit that there is some truth to it, but surely it's almost like blaming the victim to think that we're responsible for who governs us. Or is it? This is, after all, a democratic republic; what are our responsibilities?

Perhaps if we were better citizens we would get better politicians and we could have more respect for those who hold public office. We are constantly clamoring for more accountability from our government servants, but who holds *us* accountable? Is it just voting that determines good citizenship, or should there be other qualities and responsibilities used to determine how well we are holding up our end of the good-government bargain?

There is no shortage of measures, scorecards, and top-ten lists in our society. We know what our ideal weight should be, how many servings of fruits and vegetables we should eat a day, what our cholesterol and blood pressure levels should be, and on and on. Although we know very little about what it takes to be a good citizen, do we really need another test or an index so we can measure it? Despite the inherent difficulty in convincing people to take a test of their own free will, I think the answer is yes.

The Citizenship Index

A citizenship index is a good idea because the concept and responsibilities of citizenship are so important. The "criteria for good citizenship" that I offer here are from a political scientist who has spent more than thirty-five years studying the public sector, working with citizens on many projects and recommending all manner of reforms to make our governments work better. These criteria are not presented to reduce citizenship to some mathematical formula, nor to brand citizens according to how well they score. They are offered to encourage discussion and self-examination, and because our democracy is threatened when citizens are not well informed and fully engaged. We have civic obligations that extend beyond paying taxes, voting, and defending our country in case of need. An index such as the one presented here should be useful in stimulating thought about what these other obligations may be.

A couple of important caveats should be mentioned. It is certainly possible to have fewer, more, or different criteria from the ones listed here. Because this is something of a preliminary exercise, I have limited the criteria to the ten that I think are the most important or thought provoking. For ease of comparison, I have also included a numerical scale in addition to the range of responses from "very poor" to "exceptional." This is done to allow respondents to give themselves an overall score. But because the index is primarily designed to promote reflection, caution is advised in interpreting these scores. Certain of the criteria are arguably more important than others for assessing citizenship. For example, the criteria of voting, information, involvement, and accountability are generally seen as being more directly related to good citizenship than are healthy living or family harmony. Thus two identical scores of, say, 85 can mean quite different things depending on which criteria each respondent scored higher or lower on.

This index is open to a number of uses and can be adjusted to accommodate various concerns. Some people may wish to weight the criteria to reflect what certain communities or groups of voters might feel are the most important or significant criteria. Or, as I have already indicated, others might prefer to use only the first four criteria as the true test of citizenship. In distinction from these traditional measures of the political dimension of citizenship, the criteria of healthy living, civil behavior, openness, and the like can be seen as emerging issues that should be given some consideration when discussing the values and behavior of a good citizen.

Voting. The first category concerns the quality of your voting record. If you vote in every election, are familiar with the candidates' positions and voting records, and don't just vote the party line, then give yourself a high score. However, if you rarely vote, guess on many candidates, or just vote the party automatically, then give yourself a low score.

Voting Quality

Very poor		Unsatisfactory		Acceptable		Good		Exceptional	
1	2	3	4	5	6	7	8	9	10

Information. To be a good voter and a good all-around citizen, it is important to be well informed. People get information from many sources: books, magazines, electronic media, newspapers, other people, and the Internet. You should choose a high score if you spend at least a few hours every week seeking information for actual use in voting, asking questions, writing letters, or somehow influencing the political system. If you keep files on various topics, score yourself high. If you are interested in more than one issue, score yourself high as well.

Well-Informed

Very poor		Unsatisfactory		Acceptable		Good		Exceptional	
1	2	3	4	5	6	7	8	9	10

Involvement. Good citizens manage to find time for their community or to pursue some type of civic engagement. This dimension is more about commitment of time than it is about financial donations. Rate yourself high if you belong to more than one civic group or association, or if you take time to attend meetings or write letters to public officials.

Quality of Involvement

Very poor		Unsatisfactory		Acceptable		Good		Exceptional	
1	2	3	4	5	6	7	8	9	10

Accountability. Do you make a concerted effort to hold your political representatives accountable for their actions between elections? Do you e-mail them, write to them, call them, or visit them? Do you offer suggestions and take note of whether you got a meaningful response from those politicians you have contacted? Score yourself high if you contact one or more politicians at least monthly, or if you have volunteered to be part of a focus group or town hall meeting where elected persons are held accountable.

Quality of Accountability

Very poor		Unsatisfactory		Acceptable		Good		Exceptional	
1	2	3	4	5	6	7	8	9	10

Family Unit or Neighbor. We have a responsibility to ensure that our immediate family and neighbors are living in harmony and working together effectively. Rate yourself high if you regularly make time for others to help meet their needs in some way.

Family-Neighbor Harmony

Very poor		Unsatisfactory		Acceptable		Good		Exceptional	
1	2	3	4	5	6	7	8	9	10

Healthy Living. Healthy living is important not only for ourselves but also for our families, communities, and society. Part of the reason healthy living is relevant to citizenship is simply that health care is costly. Healthy living and preventive health care can reduce the need for expensive intervention later, thereby helping to reduce the overall societal level of spending on health care and making health care more affordable for others. Score yourself high if you don't smoke or drink alcohol (or do so in moderation) and if you get regular exercise and eat a healthy, balanced diet.

Attention to Health

Very poor		Unsatisfactory		Acceptable		Good		Exceptional	
1	2	3	4	5	6	7	8	9	10

Civil Behavior. Creating a civil society begins with everyone treating others with respect despite the stress many people are under. But beyond the absence of rude and possibly dangerous behavior such as road rage, a strong civil society requires positive concern with issues affecting the quality of life in the community. Rate yourself high if you practice patience and understanding; help others stay cool, calm, and collected; and encourage civil behavior and action.

Civil Behavior

Very poor		Unsatisfactory		Acceptable		Good		Exceptional	
1	2	3	4	5	6	7	8	9	10

Environmental Concern. Every citizen has a responsibility to help pass on a cleaner planet to the next generation. Are you well informed about the environmental consequences of your actions? Do you take them into account in making decisions? Give yourself a high score if you actively recycle, attempt to save energy, discourage reliance on pesticides, and use environmentally friendly products.

Environmental Concern

Very poor		Unsatisfactory		Acceptable		Good		Exceptional	
1	2	3	4	5	6	7	8	9	10

Moral and Ethical Behavior. We should hold ourselves to the same high moral and ethical standards that we expect of our politicians. The pursuit of private interest should be tempered with regard for standards of conduct that uphold the common good. Give yourself a high mark if you conscientiously act in ways that seek to balance these sometimes conflicting values.

Moral and Ethical Behavior

Very poor		Unsatisfactory		Acceptable		Good		Exceptional	
1	2	3	4	5	6	7	8	9	10

Openness. Just as no one has a monopoly on wisdom, tolerance for other points of view is not only a means of showing respect for others but a good way to learn something new as well. If you are rigid and dogmatic in your political views, then you reduce the chance of increased understanding and compromise. You should rate yourself high if you are open to differing points of view, share ideas with others in conversation, and can respect differences while still disagreeing.

Openness

Very poor		Unsatisfactory		Acceptable		Good		Exceptional	
1	2	3	4	5	6	7	8	9	10

Conclusion

The word *apathy* is overused as an excuse for or explanation of citizen disinterest in civic affairs. Pundits often delight in blaming the system or politicians themselves for low voter turnout or a low level of interest in politics. Although there is a responsibility on the part of the media and everyone in public life to encourage a high level of interest in our government, it doesn't stop there. Each of us has an individual responsibility to be a good citizen. This index highlights important dimensions of what constitutes good citizenship. The next time a politician or bureaucrat does something that infuriates you, take a moment to consider your own performance as a citizen. Maybe there are a few things you can do to become a better citizen, and in the process help to create a better society.

Charles Bens is a principal with Best Practices Consulting, a firm specializing in public sector decision making.

At a Crossroad

Gregory Maher

Growing up as a boy in Mexico, Gilberto Cetina spent hours watching his mother cook. The family operated a small *fonda*, or boardinghouse, that served Yucatanese cuisine, a delectable blend of Mexican, Spanish, and Lebanese foods. Cetina emigrated to Los Angeles in 1981. After a long span of working for others, in 1997 he launched a catering business, serving church functions and family gatherings. As the years passed, though, he never let go of his ultimate dream of opening a restaurant, but the initial capital costs proved too high and the regulation maze too hard to negotiate.

In 1999, Cetina read a flier describing a marketplace to be opened in South Central Los Angeles by a nonprofit community development corporation (CDC) called Esperanza Community Housing Corporation. He met with representatives from Esperanza and learned that in addition to developing the center, the group was to provide technical assistance and zero-interest loans to all tenants, with payments deferred during business startup. It seemed too good to be true. Yet within a few months Cetina and his partner were among the initial tenants selected for Mercado La Paloma. On February 5, 2001, his restaurant, ChichÈn-Itz·, opened its doors, specializing in Yucatanese food. The business created five permanent jobs for the community. Already he is considering expansion plans if things go well. Says Cetina, "This is the biggest change of my life, and I am very happy."

Sister Diane Donoghue founded Esperanza in 1989 and has lived in South Central since 1973. A feisty leader who knows the neighborhood's needs and resources well, she raised an enormous amount of financial and community support to make La Paloma happen. Before the mercado, Esperanza had developed 115 units of affordable housing and two child care centers, but no commercial enterprises. Typical of a community-based nonprofit, however, Esperanza identified an unmet need and pursued a solution with vigor.

La Paloma features freshly prepared foods, handmade crafts, and flowers. It gives local, low-income entrepreneurs a supportive venue to produce and sell their goods and services. The mercado is a lovely place for families to eat, shop, and attend functions. Social service organizations (a family crisis center, a housing advocacy group, and two health care referral agencies) occupy the second story. This last piece is crucial in the eyes of project manager Melanie

Stephens, who says the mercado is a "unique and respectful way of making social services available to people without having them separated from the life of the community and labeled 'in-need' . . . it pulls together the economic, artistic and social resources of the neighborhood under one roof." She said people just feel good about being there.

Urban Recovery

As the century begins, many inner-city neighborhoods in America are showing signs of recovery after years of deterioration. This revival is more than accidental; it testifies to the methodical efforts of hundreds of CDCs such as Esperanza. For forty years, they have been the workhorses of the community development movement. Early members of their ranks evolved from the community organizing drives of the 1950s. Today CDCs work to rebuild neighborhoods physically, economically, and socially. They toil in run-down places, advocate for greater public support, and battle eroding urban job bases. Despite long odds, they and their supporters—churches, government, philanthropists, and some corporations—have scored striking victories, catalyzing the rebirth of many forgotten areas.

One well-known street immediately comes to mind. By the mid-1970s, Charlotte Street in the Bronx was devastated, its buildings destroyed by arsonists and demolished. Jimmy Carter and Ronald Reagan walked the street during their presidential campaigns. Each man said it symbolized failed federal policies and promised to do better.

In 1993, Secretary of the Treasury Robert Rubin toured Charlotte Street and saw something far different. By then, the block was rebuilt with affordable homes developed by the Mid-Bronx Desperados, a neighborhood CDC. As Rubin said in a recent *Governing* magazine cover story, "the notion of community neighborhood leadership driving activity is inherently very sensible. . . . I was not aware of that until I went to the Bronx."[1]

The Ford Foundation recognized the potential of CDCs in the beginning, providing seed capital to many fledgling groups in the 1960s. Ford also created the Local Initiatives Support Corporation (LISC) in 1979. LISC is a national charity that raises money from foundations, banks, and corporations. Though burdened by a hard-to-remember name, it has grown to become the largest nonprofit organization aiding the work of CDCs, offering money, technical assistance, and policy support. It operates forty local programs in the United States; in Los Angeles it supplied a $2 million loan to La Paloma.

Rubin left Treasury in 1999 after a string of successes. To the surprise of many, his next move was to become the new chair of LISC. Community development could scarcely have hoped for a more powerful endorsement. LISC President Michael Rubinger said of Rubin, "He brings LISC and the whole community development field to a new consciousness among people who may never have heard of it."[2]

What Rubin sees now are CDCs with expanding agendas and hopes. Nationwide groups similar to Esperanza build housing and develop office, retail, and industrial space to support neighborhood businesses. Some CDCs construct space for local health care and child care facilities, and charter schools. Others focus on workforce development (the new term for job training). Most are pragmatic organizations, partnering with for-profit developers to increase development capacity and forging productive relationships with state and local government. All CDCs seek to turn isolated inner-city neighborhoods into decent places for people of modest income.

Community Renewal Tax Relief Act

For years, flat federal assistance for low-income housing and the lack of an efficient federal subsidy to support economic development have impeded even greater progress by CDCs. As the decade of the 1990s progressed, however, the Clinton administration and some members of Congress began to believe in CDCs as effective agents of change. This led in part to a significant step. In November 1999, at the urging of LISC and others, President Clinton and Speaker of the House Dennis Hastert publicly pledged to create new incentives for economic investment in the country's distressed areas. Remarkably, only a year later, they kept their promise, crafting a bipartisan bill in a lame duck congressional session. On December 21, 2000, with little notice by the media, Clinton signed his last bill as president, the Community Renewal Tax Relief Act of 2000.

The act uses a simple device, tax credits, to achieve results (an investor realizes tax savings for funds put at risk). Tax credits have grown increasingly popular as a means of implementing social policy in the United States. CDCs, government, and investors love them because they are easily administered and can be targeted to poor communities with precision. They can also be sold, creating an efficient system for the flow of investment money.

Specifically, the act expanded low-income housing tax credits (housing credits) for the first time since 1986. These credits are the remaining big tool the federal government has to finance new rental housing. Each year, demand has grown for housing credits. Because inflation has eroded their value by 40 percent, year by year worthy projects have gone begging. The new act should reverse some of that. It increases housing credits by 40 percent over two years, with inflation adjustments thereafter.

The act also created new-market tax credits, introduced by Clinton in his final State of the Union address and widely backed by Republicans. New-market tax credits establish a tax benefit for investments supporting economic development, infusing up to $15 billion of new capital into commercial projects in low-income census tracts. This in turn should increase the flow of funds to more projects like Esperanza's mercado. Rather than cobbling funds together from many places (no less than 197 in Esperanza's case), a CDC accessing new-market credits should be able to tap fewer sources. This allows a project to be completed faster and more economically. The goal is to restore commerce and create jobs—two essential ingredients in returning a low-income area to health.

This boost to community development comes just in time. Too many Americans still cannot afford decent housing. According to a recent National Low Income Housing Coalition study entitled "Out of Reach," the national median housing wage for a two-bedroom apartment now stands at $12.47 an hour, more than double the federal minimum wage of $5.15 an hour. In the next five years, one million subsidized housing units will lose rent restrictions because of expiring insurance and Section 8 contracts administered by the U.S. Department of Housing and Urban Development. Jobs, particularly those paying a living wage, remain unavailable, or geographically too far away, for many residents. Moreover, it is difficult to employ scores of inner-city inhabitants because they have personal or social problems or skill gaps, or are unable to find child care.

Yet some optimism is justified by the act. More economic vitality in disinvested areas should return them to being safe ground for further renewal. Moving the new act through partisan waters also required difficult work. This should be a beacon, and a model, for President Bush, who has pledged a reach-across-the-aisle approach to solving national problems. CDCs, and the people they serve, have reason to be hopeful.

Note

1. Swope, C. "Robert Rubin's Urban Crusade." *Governing,* 2000, *13*(11), 24.
2. Swope (2000), p. 20.

Gregory Maher is vice president and deputy general counsel of the Local Initiatives Support Corporation.

ORDERING INFORMATION

MAIL ORDERS TO:
  Jossey-Bass
  350 Sansome Street
  San Francisco, CA 94104-1342

PHONE subscription or single-copy orders toll-free at (888) 378-2537 or at (415) 433-1767 (toll call).

FAX orders toll-free to: (800) 605-2665

SUBSCRIPTIONS cost $50.00 for individuals U.S./Canada/Mexico; $83.00 for U.S. for institutions, agencies, and libraries; $123.00 for Canada institutions; $157.00 for international institutions. Standing orders are accepted. (For subscriptions outside the United States, orders must be prepaid in U.S. dollars by check drawn on a U.S. bank or charged to VISA, MasterCard, American Express, or Discover.)

SINGLE COPIES cost $23.00 plus shipping (see below) when payment accompanies order. Please include appropriate sales tax. Canadian residents, add GST and any local taxes. Billed orders will be charged shipping and handling. No billed shipments to Post Office boxes. (Orders from outside the United States must be prepaid in U.S. dollars drawn on a U.S. bank or charged to VISA, MasterCard, or American Express.)

Prices are subject to change without notice.

SHIPPING (single copies only): $30.00 and under, add $5.50; $30.01 to $50.00, add $6.50; $50.01 to $75.00, add $8.00; $75.01 to $100.00, add $10.00; $100.01 to $150.00, add $12.00. Call for information on overnight delivery or shipments outside the United States.

ALL ORDERS must include either the name of an individual or an official purchase order number. Please submit your orders as follows:
  Subscriptions: specify issue (for example, NCR 86:1) you would like subscription to begin with.
  Single copies: specify volume and issue number. Available from Volume 86 onward. For earlier issues, see below.

MICROFILM available from University Microfilms, 300 North Zeeb Road, Ann Arbor, MI 48106. Back issues through Volume 85 and bound volumes available from William S. Hein & Co., 1285 Main Street, Buffalo, NY 14209. Full text available in the electronic versions of the Social Sciences Index, H. W. Wilson Co., 950 University Avenue, Bronx, NY 10452, and in CD-ROM from EBSCO Publishing, 83 Pine Street, P.O. Box 2250, Peabody, MA 01960. The full text of individual articles is available via fax modem through Uncover Company, 3801 East Florida Avenue, Suite 200, Denver, CO 80210. For bulk reprints (50 or more), call Gabriela Solorzano, Jossey-Bass, at (415) 433-1740.

DISCOUNTS FOR QUANTITY ORDERS are available. For information, please write to Jossey-Bass, 350 Sansome Street, San Francisco, CA 94104-1342.

LIBRARIANS are encouraged to write to Jossey-Bass for a free sample issue.

VISIT THE JOSSEY-BASS HOME PAGE on the World Wide Web at http://www.josseybass.com for an order form or information about other titles of interest.

National Civic League Officers and Directors

2001 Officers
Chair, Dorothy Ridings, Council on Foundations, Washington, D.C.
Vice Chairman, David Vidal, The Conference Board, New York
Treasurer, James D. Howard, Century Pacific, Phoenix, Arizona
Secretary, Carrie Thornhill, D.C. Agenda, Washington, D.C.
President, Christopher T. Gates, Denver
Assistant Treasurer, John W. Amberg, Denver

Board of Directors
D. David Altman, The Murray and Agnes Seasongood Good Government
    Foundation, Cincinnati, Ohio
John Claypool, Greater Philadelphia First, Philadelphia
Patricia Edwards, National Center for Community Education, Flint, Michigan
Badi G. Foster, Tufts University, Medford, Massachusetts
Dr. J. Eugene Grigsby, III, University of California, Los Angeles
Hubert Guest, Cheverly, Maryland
Dr. John Stuart Hall, Arizona State University, Phoenix
Dr. Lenneal J. Henderson, Jr., University of Baltimore, Baltimore, Maryland
Dr. Theodore Hershberg, University of Pennsylvania, Philadelphia
Curtis Johnson, The CitiStates Group, St. Paul, Minnesota
Anna Faith Jones, Boston Foundation, Boston
Dr. David Mathews, Kettering Foundation, Dayton, Ohio
Robert H. Muller, J.P. Morgan Securities, New York
Sylvester Murray, Cleveland State University, Cleveland
Betty Jane Narver, University of Washington, Seattle
Frank J. Quevedo, Southern California Edison, Rosemead, California
Robert Rawson, Jr., Jones, Day, Reavis & Pogue, Cleveland
Juan Sepulveda, The Common Enterprise, San Antonio, Texas
Arturo Vargas, NALEO Educational Fund, Los Angeles
Linda Wong, Community Development Technologies Center, Los Angeles

Honorary Life Directors and Former Chairmen
Terrell Blodgett, Austin, Texas
Hon. Bill Bradley, Newark, New Jersey
Hon. Henry Cisneros, Los Angeles
Hon. R. Scott Fosler, Washington, D.C.
Hon. John W. Gardner, Stanford, California
James L. Hetland, Jr., Minneapolis, Minnesota
Hon. George Latimer, St. Paul, Minnesota
Hon. William W. Scranton, Scranton, Pennsylvania
Hon. William F. Winter, Jackson, Mississippi

ALL PRICES include shipping and handling (for orders outside the United States, please add $15 for shipping). National Civic League members receive a 10 percent discount. Bulk rates are available. See end of this list for ordering information.

Most Frequently Requested Publications

The Civic Index: A New Approach to Improving Community Life
National Civic League staff, 1993
50 pp., 7 × 10 paper, $7.00

The Community Visioning and Strategic Planning Handbook
National Civic League staff, 1995
53 pp., $23.00

Governance

National Report on Local Campaign Finance Reform
New Politics Program staff, 1998
96 pp., $15.00

Communities and the Voting Rights Act
National Civic League staff, 1996
118 pp., 8.5 × 11 paper, $12.00

Forms of Local Government
National Civic League staff, 1993
15 pp., 5.5 × 8.5 pamphlet, $3.00

Guide for Charter Commissions (Fifth Edition)
National Civic League staff, 1991
46 pp., 6 × 9 paper, $10.00

Handbook for Council Members in Council-Manager Cities (Fifth Edition)
National Civic League staff, 1992
38 pp., 6 × 9 paper, $12.00

Measuring City Hall Performance: Finally, A How-To Guide
Charles K. Bens, 1991
127 pp., 8.5 × 11 monograph, $15.00

Model County Charter (Revised Edition)
National Civic League staff, 1990
53 pp., 5.5 × 8.5 paper, $10.00

Modern Counties: Professional Management—The Non-Charter Route
National Civic League staff, 1993
54 pp., paper, $8.00

Term Limitations for Local Officials: A Citizen's Guide to Constructive Dialogue
Laurie Hirschfeld Zeller, 1992
24 pp., 5.5 × 8.5 pamphlet, $3.00

Using Performance Measurement in Local Government: A Guide to Improving Decisions, Performance, and Accountability
   Paul D. Epstein, 1988
   225 pp., 6 × 9 paper, $5.00

Model City Charter (Seventh Edition)
   National Civic League staff, 1997
   110 pp., 5.5 × 8.5 monograph, $14.00

Alliance for National Renewal

ANR Community Resource Manual
   National Civic League Staff, 1996
   80 pp., 8.5 × 11, $6.00

Taking Action: Building Communities That Strengthen Families
   Special section in *Governing Magazine,* 1998
   8 pp., 8.5 × 11 (color), $3.00

Communities That Strengthen Families
   Insert in *Governing Magazine,* 1997
   8 pp., 8.5 × 11 reprint, $3.00

Connecting Government and Neighborhoods
   Insert in *Governing Magazine,* 1996
   8 pp., 8.5 × 11 reprint, $3.00

The Culture of Renewal
   Richard Louv, 1996
   45 pp., $8.00

The Kitchen Table
   Quarterly newsletter of Alliance for National Renewal, 1999
   8 pp., annual subscription (4 issues) $12.00, free to ANR Partners

The Landscape of Civic Renewal
   Civic renewal projects and studies from around the country, 1999
   185 pp., $12.00

National Renewal
   John W. Gardner, 1995
   27 pp., 7 × 10, $7.00

San Francisco Civic Scan
   Richard Louv, 1996
   100 pp., $6.00

1998 Guide to the Alliance for National Renewal
   National Civic League staff, 1998
   50 pp., 4 × 9, $5.00

Springfield, Missouri: A Nice Community Wrestles with How to Become a Good Community
   Alliance for National Renewal staff, 1996
   13 pp., $7.00

Toward a Paradigm of Community-Making
  Allan Wallis, 1996
  60 pp., $12.00

The We Decade: Rebirth on Community
  Dallas Morning News, 1995
  39 pp., 8.5 × 14 reprint, $3.00

99 Things You Can Do for Your Community in 1999
  poster (folded), $6.00

Healthy Communities

Healthy Communities Handbook
  National Civic League staff, 1993
  162 pp., 8.5 × 11 monograph, $22.00

All-America City Awards

All-America City Yearbook (1991, 1992, 1993, 1994, 1995, 1996, 1997)
  National Civic League staff
  60 pp., 7 × 10 paper, $4.00 shipping and handling

All-America City Awards Audio Tape Briefing
  Audiotape, $4.00 shipping and handling

Diversity and Regionalism

Governance and Diversity:
Findings from Oakland, 1995
Findings from Fresno, 1995
Findings from Los Angeles, 1994
  National Civic League staff
  7 × 10 paper, $5.00 each

Networks, Trust and Values
  Allan D. Wallis, 1994
  51 pp., 7 × 10 paper, $7.00

Inventing Regionalism
  Allan D. Wallis, 1995
  75 pp., 8.5 × 11 monograph, $19.00

Leadership, Collaboration, and Community Building

Citistates: How Urban America Can Prosper in a Competitive World
  Neal Peirce, Curtis Johnson, and John Stuart Hall, 1993
  359 pp., 6.5 × 9.5, $25.00

Collaborative Leadership
  David D. Chrislip and Carl E. Larson, 1994
  192 pp., 6 × 9.5, $20.00

Good City and the Good Life
  Daniel Kemmis, 1995
  226 pp., 6 × 8.5, $23.00

On Leadership
  John W. Gardner, 1990
  220 pp., 6 × 9.5, $28.00

Politics for People: Finding a Responsible Public Voice
  David Mathews, 1994
  229 pp., 6 × 9.5, $20.00

Public Journalism and Public Life
  David "Buzz" Merritt, 1994
  129 pp., 6 × 9, $30.00

Resolving Municipal Disputes
  David Stiebel, 1992
  2 audiotapes and book, $15.00

Time Present, Time Past
  Bill Bradley, former chairman of the National Civic League, 1996
  450 pp., paper, $13.00

Transforming Politics
  David D. Chrislip, 1995
  12 pp., 7 × 10, $3.00

Revolution of the Heart
  Bill Shore, 1996
  167 pp., 8.5 × 5.75, $8.00

The Web of Life
  Richard Louv, 1996
  258 pp., 7.5 × 5.5, $15.00

Programs for Community Problem Solving

Systems Reform and Local Government: Improving Outcomes for Children, Families, and Neighborhoods
  1998, 47 pp., $12.00

Building Community: Exploring the Role of Social Capital and Local Government
  1998, 31 pp., $12.00

The Transformative Power of Governance: Strengthening Community Capacity to Improve Outcomes for Children, Families, and Neighborhoods
  1998, 33 pp., $12.00

Building the Collaborative Community
  Jointly published by the National Civic League and the National Institute for Dispute Resolution, 1994
  33 pp., $12.00

Negotiated Approaches to Environmental Decision Making in Communities: An Exploration of Lessons Learned
  Jointly published by the National Institute for Dispute Resolution and the Coalition to Improve Management in State and Local Government, 1996
  58 pp., $14.00

Community Problem Solving Case Summaries, Volume III
    1992, 52 pp., $19.00

Facing Racial and Cultural Conflicts: Tools for Rebuilding Community (Second Edition)
    1994, $24.00

Collaborative Transportation Planning Guidelines for Implementing ISTEA and the CAAA
    1993, 87 pp., $14.00

Collaborative Planning Video
    Produced by the American Planning Association, 1995
    6-hr. video and 46 pp. workshop materials, $103.00

Pulling Together: A Land Use and Development Consensus Building Manual
    A joint publication of PCPS and the Urban Land Institute, 1994
    145 pp., $34.00

Solving Community Problems by Consensus
    1990, 20 pp., $14.00

Involving Citizens in Community Decision Making: A Guidebook
    1992, 30 pp., $30.00

NATIONAL CIVIC LEAGUE sales policies: Orders must be paid in advance by check, VISA, or MasterCard. We are unable to process exchanges, returns, credits, or refunds. For orders outside the United States, add $15 for shipping.

TO PLACE AN ORDER:

CALL the National Civic League at (303) 571–4343 or (800) 223–6004, or

MAIL ORDERS TO:
    National Civic League
    1445 Market Street, Suite 300
    Denver, CO 80202–1717, or

E-MAIL the National Civic League at ncl@ncl.org